PALO ALTO REMEMBERED

STORIES
FROM
A
CITY'S
PAST

PALO ALTO REMEMBERED

STORIES FROM A CITY'S PAST

MATT BOWLING

Palo Alto Historical Association
Palo Alto, California
2012

Published by the Palo Alto Historical Association
P.O. Box 193
Palo Alto, California 94302

© 2012 by Matt Bowling

Earlier versions of many of these stories appeared in the *Palo Alto Daily News* during the years 2007–2008. With permission from the *Palo Alto Daily News,* they are revised and updated for this book. Unless noted beside the image, photographs are from the Palo Alto Historical Association's Guy Miller Archives. The title page photo is by Carolyn Caddes.

All rights reserved by the Palo Alto Historical Association. No part of this book may be reproduced in any form, electronic or mechanical, without permission of the publisher.

Editor-in-chief, Betty Gerard
Image curator, Brian George
Book design, Harriette Shakes

ISBN 978-0-9638098-0-3
Printed by Omega Printing
Palo Alto, California

To my Baby Bee, Addie Luna—You make every day special.

—MB

Foreword

THE PALO ALTO HISTORICAL ASSOCIATION IS PLEASED TO PUBLISH THIS COLLECTION OF Palo Alto stories by Matt Bowling. Each story is a delightful example of Matt's storytelling skills. Most of the stories previously appeared in the *Palo Alto Daily News* during the years 2007–2008. We thank the newspaper for allowing us to publish them in this collection. Some of the stories have been written just for this book, and others have been revised or updated to some extent to reflect changes in the Palo Alto community since the story originally appeared in print.

The Palo Alto Historical Association has a long history of writing and publishing books on local history. Beginning in the 1950s, we have produced booklets on numerous topics such as schools, Indians and Spanish explorers. Our history of *Mayfield* was published in 1976 and reprinted twice. The books *Streets of Palo Alto* and *Parks of Palo Alto* continue to be popular in their revised editions.

We published the comprehensive *Centennial History of Palo Alto* for the City's 100-year celebration in 1994. It took a team of researchers, writers and editors more than six years to complete the book. It has recently gone out of print.

Matt's book is a different kind of history book. It is a collection of tasty treats rather than a full-course meal. While some readers may read the book cover-to-cover, it is designed to welcome the reader who wants to jump in and read only a story or two at a time. The individual stories stand alone and certainly do not need to be read in any specific order. There are stories from several decades, involving Palo Altans from different neighborhoods who participated in a wide range of historic events.

As a reader of local history, I have enjoyed Matt's stories, especially for the way that he connects local history to events beyond Palo Alto. All too often local history writers fail to make the association between the lives of the people in their community to what was happening on the larger stage of state, national or international events. In each of his stories, Matt does a masterful job of placing the Palo Alto story in its broader context, showing how Palo Altans of the past reacted to a time and events so unlike those of today. Too often we study history in a vacuum, with world history in one class, American history in another, with perhaps additional exposure to art history or music appreciation. Seldom was there an attempt to link all of these histories. Matt and his stories present some of those links. President Eisenhower's plan for the interstate highway system; the United States Supreme Court's decision on obscenity; or the Japanese attack on Pearl Harbor all had their impact on people and events in Palo Alto. And Matt's stories examine our local community's reaction to the broader history.

Steve Staiger
Palo Alto Historian

Acknowledgments

I WANT TO THANK THE PALO ALTO HISTORICAL ASSOCIATION FOR MAKING THIS BOOK possible. PAHA is a first-class organization full of devoted volunteers whose quest is to bring history alive in a very special city. Palo Alto's past is not simply the town records of yet another suburb somewhere between San Jose and San Francisco. Since its founding, Palo Alto has had a unique place in the Bay Area and the nation. It began in the final years of the Old West, subsequently growing into a college town, commuter suburb, hippie enclave, Silicon Valley capital—and recently—into a kind of intellectual and educational mecca. PAHA's mission has been to chronicle this amazing story through both traditional means and more recently, online. The members of the organization do so in a way that can only be called exemplary. In my view, few historical organizations display the dedication and savvy which this one does and I'm proud to be one of its members.

I also would like to single out some individuals for their yeoman efforts in this enterprise. First, a special thanks to Steve Staiger, Palo Alto's historian. Since I began this project in 2006, Steve has spent countless hours in the archives helping me, guiding me and setting me on the right course. His knowledge of Palo Alto goes far beyond facts and figures. He puts what happened in Palo Alto's past into a larger historical context, allowing one to see how the pieces fit together. On many evenings during his shifts at the History Desk at Palo Alto's main library, he and I would talk and talk about Palo Alto and years past, darting from one topic to another as we found ourselves absorbed in our favorite subject. So many thanks to Steve for all his help. I could never have written this book without him.

Also big thanks to two Board members who spent hours editing this book simply out of their devotion to PAHA and this project. Bardy Wallace and Betty Gerard made all the corrections, word changes and edits that are essential to the success of any large book. Many thanks to them for their time and effort! I'd also like to credit Brian George, Chris Botsford, Mary Beth Lefebvre, Beth Bunnenberg and PAHA President Doug Graham for their leadership and research for this book. Many of the great postcards, old photographs and newspaper stories seen here were dug up by these folks in the archives. They also provided the leadership which allowed this project to succeed. Thank you to Harriette Shakes, our designer, whose wonderful work is on full display in the pages beyond. In addition, she headed the Publications Committee and brought the book to completion, then worked closely with the marketing team on its introduction.

A special thanks to Dick Rosenbaum, former Palo Alto Mayor and PAHA President. In the early 1970s Dick helped keep Palo Alto's essence by almost single-handedly rallying Palo Altans to reject the bloated "Superblock" project downtown. It was a turning point in the city's history that I believe helped lead to the wonderful Palo Alto we all know today. Dick was also the first one to single out my work and invite me into the PAHA circle—an act which propelled me to do this project. Incidentally, he also runs the most efficient meeting I have ever seen! I really appreciate his help. A huge thank you to Veronica Marin who was the first reader of every story I have ever written about Palo Alto—and always the best audience. And finally to Addie Luna Bowling, always my inspiration.

Matt Bowling
February 2012

CONTENTS PALO ALTO REMEMBERED: STORIES FROM A CITY'S PAST

Foreword *ix*

Acknowledgments *xi*

LANDMARKS

EL PALO ALTO, Rooted in History 19

THE STANFORD THEATRE, As Time Goes By 25

DINAH'S SHACK, A Delicate History 29

UNIVERSITY AVENUE TRAIN DEPOT, A Streamline to the Past 33

THE HUMANE SOCIETY, A History of Compassion 37

STANFORD RESEARCH PARK, The Engine of Silicon Valley 41

STANFORD SHOPPING CENTER, Turning Pastures into Profits 45

THE WINTER LODGE, Skating Through the Political Process 49

THE BOL PARK DONKEYS, Neighborhood Pets 53

LONG AGO

THE 1906 EARTHQUAKE, "Like a Terrier Shaking a Rat" 57

PALO ALTO'S EARLY FIRES, Fearing the Flames 63

THE FOURTH OF JULY, Summertime Celebrations 67

THE CIRCUS, The Greatest Show in Palo Alto 71

THE HOTEL DE ZINK, A Friend Indeed   75
MARCH 13, 1939, A Day in the Life   79
PALO ALTO'S CIVIL DEFENSE, Panic After Pearl Harbor   83
THE PALO ALTO HOME FRONT, Life During Wartime   87
THE PALO ALTO DRIVE-IN, A Generational Memory   93

CHANGING TIMES

PATERNALISM AT THE MOVIES, Palo Alto's Commercial Board of Amusements   97
WOOLWORTH'S, Palo Alto's Five and Dime   101
RESTAURANT ROW, Some Good Ol' Palo Alto Cooking   105
A DELIVERY FROM THE PAST, Palo Alto's Milkmen   109
THE PARIS THEATRE, Prurience or Porno-Chic?   113
BIKES IN PALO ALTO, A Ride Through History   117
THE CUBBERLEY CLOSING, A Tough Call   121

CONFLICTS

SAVE THE OAKS! Palo Alto's First Environmental Victory   125
THE KKK IN PALO ALTO, Terror vs Tolerance   129
THE EMBARCADERO UNDERPASS, Accident Before Action   133
JAPANESE-AMERICAN INTERNMENT, Palo Alto's Deported Patriots   137
HOUSING DISCRIMINATION, A Closed Door in Palo Alto   143

THE OREGON EXPRESSWAY, Residentialists Unite   149

THE 1967 RECALL ELECTION, Palo Alto's Political Rumble   153

VENCEREMOS, Arming for a Fight   157

CLOSING THE YACHT HARBOR, The Battle by the Bay   161

CITIZENS

ANNA ZSCHOKKE, The Mother of Palo Alto's Schools   167

BIRGE CLARK, An Architectural Legacy   171

JFK AT STANFORD, Days of Decision   175

WILLIAM SHOCKLEY, "Paranoia Strikes Deep…"   179

RUSSEL V. A. LEE, It's a Wonderful Life   183

THE GRATEFUL DEAD, Making the Scene in Palo Alto   187

BEATLEMANIA INVADES PALO ALTO, A Celebrity Story   191

JIM ZURCHER, Chief Superpig   195

GREG BROWN: MURALS & PUBLIC ART, Fueling the Imagination in Palo Alto   199

MORE

About the Author   205

The Palo Alto Historical Association   207

LANDMARKS

A train passes the twin-trunked El Palo Alto at the San Francisquito Creek crossing, 1864. [DRAWING: YISCHER]

EL PALO ALTO
Rooted in History

Every great city deserves a great symbol—some sort of natural landmark or iconic structure that looks good on the city letterhead and in tourist brochures while still recalling the city's roots and history. The Statue of Liberty, Eiffel Tower and Golden Gate Bridge are all man-made structures that represent proud cities in their most idyllic glory. But while Palo Alto is a lot smaller than the sprawling metropolises of New York, Paris or San Francisco, it has a city symbol with just as much grace and dignity. This is the story of California's oldest living landmark, the tree known as El Palo Alto.

Actually, to fully tell that story you have to go back more than 1,000 years. El Palo Alto, the tall redwood that stands near Palo Alto's northern border, has been rooted to that spot for a millennium. It's an amazing fact to consider. Today tree lovers can walk into a small park on the banks of San Francisquito Creek and look up at this enormous redwood that was just a small sapling when Leif Ericsson first set foot in the Americas. Indeed, El Palo Alto was past 500 years old when Christopher Columbus set sail and it was nearing its 800th birthday in 1769 when most historians believe Don Gaspar de Portolà and his band of explorers first "discovered" the tree while looking for Monterey Bay.

Of course, if you visit El Palo Alto today, it's difficult to get a sense of the landmark status it enjoyed in those early days of California exploration. Now it's just one of many redwoods, oaks and non-native trees clustered near the railroad tracks along the Menlo Park border. But part of what makes El Palo Alto a perfect city emblem is that it transports one back to an earlier era when all that stood between the mountains and the bay were undisturbed grassy slopes and fields. A time when El Palo Alto was the tallest tree for miles around.

Don Gaspar de Portolà "discovered" El Palo Alto in 1769 while looking for Monterey Bay. [WIKIPEDIA COMMONS/PAINTED C. 1770]

EL PALO ALTO THROUGH TIME—ROOTED IN HISTORY

1875
Twin trunked El Palo Alto before a storm reduced it to one trunk.

1890
El Palo Alto with a single trunk.

20

1951
A train passes a rather scraggly looking El Palo Alto.

1963
In this photo, El Palo's trunk looks almost entirely exposed.

2007
A train passes a healthier-looking El Palo Alto.

The Native Sons of the Golden West honoring what they thought was a dying tree, 1926.

In those days, El Palo Alto had twin trunks standing side by side. One twin would succumb to a mid-1880s windstorm, but a photo taken a decade earlier records the distinctive character of the twin tree that on a clear day could be seen from San Francisco. Mrs. C. F. de Ramirez recalled approaching El Palo Alto in the early days. As a little girl in 1837, she first saw the twin trunks from the hills in Belmont. She remembered that "it was a clear day and as we topped the summit of the hill, I saw the two noble trees, intertwined like brothers towering high above the oaks and buckeyes. In those days the twin redwoods were indeed beautiful trees, green and stately."

Portolà's chief scout, Sergeant Ortega, must have seen it much the same way nearly 70 years earlier when he viewed the two tall trees from the high mountains near present-day San Carlos. The Portolà explorers had come up from San Diego in 1769 searching for Monterey Bay. But as early explorers had a tendency to do, Portola's band got lost and found something else of significance—the San Francisco Bay. As the procession struggled down the hills they used the twin trees as a guide—later camping beneath El Palo Alto between November 6th and 11th of 1769.

The twin trees that the Spanish called Palos Colorados (red trees) and later El Palo Alto (the tall tree) also served as a guide to other explorers. After camping beside the tree, Fra Pedro Font included El Palo Alto on his 1770 topographical map of San Francisco. "I beheld in the distance a tree of immense stature rising above the plain of oaks like a grand tower," he wrote in his diary upon first seeing the twin redwoods. And in 1776, Padre Francisco erected a cross beneath El Palo Alto to mark a proposed mission site, although Spanish engineers and military strategists in San Francisco eventually decided to build the mission in Santa Clara.

In later years, the city of Palo Alto would grow up under the scraggly branches of El Palo Alto. A century after the Spanish explorers took note of the tall tree, Senator Leland Stanford settled trotting horses on his new Palo Alto Stock Farm. Later he and his wife Jane founded a university that would model El Palo Alto on its official seal. And as the University Park tract matured around Stanford University, it incorporated in 1894 as the city of Palo Alto. The new city was already a stopping point for the Southern Pacific Railroad, which had laid its track lines beneath the natural landmark. The train depot less than a half-mile south at University Avenue became known to many as Big Tree Station.

Despite fondness for El Palo Alto, the tree has been in danger since it was first sighted from that hilltop. Poisonous train smoke and emerging farms certainly didn't do the tree much good.

Still, it was nature that did the most damage to El Palo Alto. During a particularly harsh winter in the mid-1880s, the tall tree lost its weaker half in a violent wind storm. When it came down, locals eagerly counted the rings and found the downed redwood to be 960 years old.

By the mid-1920s, many feared that El Palo Alto's days were numbered. Issuing a kind of last rite, the local Native Sons of the Golden West hurried to honor El Palo Alto in 1926—presenting it with a bronze plaque set in a granite boulder. But thanks to help over the years, first from Leland and Jane Stanford and later from the city of Palo Alto and local caregivers, great effort has been taken to preserve this hearty landmark. Soil and mulch have been filled in near the tree's base, dead limbs are periodically cut off, spraying is done to combat tree pests, and a pipe runs up its trunk bringing water to mist the treetop.

Having weathered the railroad, loggers, floods, termites, wind storms and smog, El Palo Alto still stands along San Francisquito Creek towering over the city and refusing to die. So if ever you find yourself near venerable El Palo Alto, stop and give that old tree a hug. After all, it's earned it.

Looking up at the pipe that brings the misting system to El Palo Alto's upper regions, 2007.
[PHOTO: MATT BOWLING]

David Woodley Packard poses in the balcony of the newly restored Stanford Theatre. [PENINSULA TIMES TRIBUNE/VERN FISHER]

THE STANFORD THEATRE
As Time Goes By

For a time in its history it seemed that the Stanford Theatre, Palo Alto's oldest and grandest movie house, would suffer the unfortunate fate of most single-screen theatres of yesteryear. As cable and color television, VCRs and year-round TV sports lured people to stay home on Friday and Saturday nights—and big screen multiplexes opened within a short freeway drive—the Stanford began to sink ever further down the cinematic food chain, eventually showing second-run Hollywood action flicks while remaining poised on the verge of being eaten up by shops and restaurants.

But thanks to the David and Lucile Packard Foundation and the zeal of the billionaire's son, movie buff David Woodley Packard, the story of the Stanford has a happy ending after all. It just goes to show what a little vision and $8 million can do.

But no matter how high the price tag for the theatre's restoration and operation, today the Stanford is one of Palo Alto's treasures, sending lines of patrons around the block for "Casablanca," "Citizen Kane" and the annual Christmas Eve showing of "It's a Wonderful Life." Indeed, it's the Stanford that gives Palo Alto the same kind of small-town charm that inspired George Bailey to run down Main Street calling out his hellos to Bedford Falls.

The Stanford—or New Stanford as it was then known—was built in 1925 for $300,000, replacing its predecessor as part of the Peninsula Theatre Company chain. It was immediately billed in the local papers as "The pride of the Peninsula,… the last word in theatre construction." As one of the finest movie houses in California in its early years, it featured the most modern amenities of the day. A "mushroom" ventilation system allowed for even temperature control throughout

The restored Stanford Theatre marquee.
[THE CAROLYN PIERCE POSTCARD COLLECTION.]

This photograph was taken just before the Stanford Theatre's grand opening, June 9, 1925.

the theatre, a "remote control" switchboard system operated the lights and curtain from the projection booth and the Stanford claimed an enormous seating capacity of 1,443.

And that's about how many came on the evening of June 9, 1925, when the Stanford opened with a showing of comedian Reginald Denny's "I'll Show You the Town," highlighted by an appearance by the star himself and an address by the mayor. The Stanford also hosted "high-class vaudeville" acts in its early days, giving Palo Alto a venue for popular culture during the Depression. For the next four decades, the Stanford would be the place to see local premieres of such classics as "The Philadelphia Story," "Gone with the Wind" and "Rear Window"—along with the requisite Fox "Movietone News" and "Talkartoons."

But by the late 1960s, the Stanford was no longer drawing the big crowds. For a time, it became a performing arts theatre, hosting off-off Broadway shows and classic musicals like "Oklahoma!" and "South Pacific" as well as fading pop acts like "Tower of Power." Such experiments soon led to financial disaster and it all ended up with a "For Sale" sign up on the marquee.

By the early 1980s, the Stanford was playing movies again, but of a second-run variety. You could see Hollywood blockbusters months after their release. And if you were willing to put up with the Stanford's peeling paint and rusted seats, you could get in for 50 cents—a dime less than the price of a film when the theatre first opened nearly six decades earlier.

But just as it looked as if the Stanford's days were numbered, a white knight came forth in the person of David Woodley Packard. Although the onetime classics professor had not been interested in film until the age of 35 when a friend took him to see the "Wizard of Oz," Packard had since developed a nearly fanatical passion for the fate of old movies. In 1987, he rented out the Stanford for a week to serenade friends with a fortnight of Fred Astaire pictures. The results were phenomenal. More than a 1,000 people lined up each night to see Fred and Ginger dance cheek to cheek. Packard began to flirt with the idea of buying the Stanford and when his old man came by and saw the crowds, the elder Packard gave his assent to the plan.

David threw himself into the restoration project. Using old photographs and company file notes, he and his crew were able to reconstruct the Stanford's glory days. Back were the original Greek-Assyrian paintings on the theatre's 50 foot ceiling. Also restored were the handmade stair tiles, seven chandeliers, stage pillars, urns and the theatre's *pièce de résistance*—the Mighty Wurlitzer organ that ascends and descends into the orchestra pit. Even the theatre's original snack bar and ticket booth were replicated with complete accuracy. In the end, it took less time (and a lot less money) to build the theatre in the first place than to do the painstaking restoration.

In the years since, the Stanford has become a place where classics are both shown and saved. Packard has close ties to the UCLA film archive, maintaining his own preservation lab on the UCLA grounds. There he has helped convert—at $10,000 apiece—many films whose only prints were previously at risk on unstable and highly flammable nitrate stock. Such new prints have often premiered at the Stanford. Still, sometimes Packard's love for the old cinema can impair his sense of what will turn a profit. After all, it's probably only the die-hard classics fans who are lining up to for tickets to Harold Lloyd film festivals.

But Packard was correct in predicting that there was a stable audience in town for Hollywood's Golden Age—and not just among the blue-haired set. More people saw the 50th anniversary re-release of "Casablanca" at the Stanford than anywhere else in the country and over the last decade the theatre has accounted for a remarkable 25 percent of the nationwide attendance of classic films. And for the local movie *aficionado*, it is a distinct pleasure to have a place in town where you can rock back in a red wool mohair seat, dig into a box of popcorn and follow the Yellow Brick Road.

Today, replicated with complete accuracy, Stanford Theatre's lobby looks almost exactly as it did in this old photo of the original.

DINAH'S SHACK AT PALO ALTO, CALIFORNIA
½ *Spring Chicken on Toast - 50c*

An 1931 postcard of Dinah's Shack. [COURTESY OF THE CAROLYN PIERCE POSTCARD COLLECTION.]

DINAH'S SHACK
A Delicate History

This old Dinah's ad reflects both the racial caricatures and dinner prices of another era. [PALO ALTO TIMES]

ANY STORY THAT PORTRAYS RACIAL ATTITUDES OF PAST GENERATIONS RAISES QUESTIONS that deserve a hard look—even in these generally more enlightened times. Our country's first leaders founded one of history's great nations. They also perpetuated slavery and many kept slaves themselves. Our constitution has proved to be a brilliant and reliable document. It also counted each black man as 3/5th of a person. Abraham Lincoln freed the slaves and was certainly progressive for his day—yet he was plainly on record in opposition to equality for blacks. When historians tell stories that reveal intolerance, how prominently should such prejudices be featured? Are these attitudes simply footnotes in history or are they the story themselves?

Such questions arise in Palo Alto's history in connection with one of its most celebrated restaurants, Dinah's Shack. While the restaurant's history ran for more than six decades, it's hard today to look back on its conspicuous mammy logo, black stable-boy statues, and other slavery-era paraphernalia without feeling more than a little uncomfortable. And while the history of Dinah's Shack tells the story of an extraordinary restaurant, it's hard not to think that the more significant story here—at least in a larger historical context—is of its paternalistic and stereotypical symbols and the blindness of whites who could not see their significance.

Dinah's Shack actually began with a tribute to a black woman. In 1926, during a horse and buggy ride down El Camino Real, the old State Highway, Charles McMonagle and his wife Hazel saw an old ramshackle structure. According to legend, Hazel cried out, "It's Dinah's Shack!"—the home of the beloved black woman who had cared for her in her Kansas childhood. The McMonagles decided to buy the shack and turn it into a roadside carry-out restaurant catering to the many highway travelers on their way back and forth from San Francisco.

John Rickey poses with Chef Fred Aebelhard beside a table covered with dishes from Dinah's famed smorgasbord (circa mid-1950s).
[PENINSULA LIVING/ROBERT H. COX]

In the early days, the restaurant was staffed almost entirely by black cooks and waiters, many of them former sleeping car porters, lured off the Southern Pacific. Dinah's Shack featured the cuisine of the South, largely African-American influenced—Southern-fried chicken on toast, biscuits and honey, waffle potatoes—as well as musical acts such as Lou Foote and his Two Toes. Between the 1920s and 1950s, Dinah's became a nationally famous stop along the old highway, known for "authentic southern hospitality," as well as for being a favorite hangout for better-off Stanford students like John F. Kennedy, who was attending the business school in the fall of 1940.

And when the entire restaurant, save the chimney, burned down in May 1942, the McMonagles managed to reopen within 48 hours in another shack—perhaps not quite like Dinah's, but still on the property lot. Eight years later, they sold to John Rickey, the hotel owner and restaurateur who owned Rickey's Garden Hotel down the street. Rickey brought a new layer of food and culture to the now 20-year-old restaurant. So-called Continental cuisine was featured in a "smorgasbord" with a Scandinavian influence. While Dinah's down-home cooking remained, it now shared the menu with Roast Duck L'Orange, Veal Cordon Bleu, and Salmon Dijonais—not to mention other smorgasbord appetizers, including marinated pig's feet and pickled herring.

Under Rickey's tenure, Dinah's was remembered warmly for many things, including dependable traditions. For instance, Phyllis Schlomovitz was a world-renowned harpist who served as Dinah's nightly entertainment for nearly 20 years. Many still remember Winnie Coughlin, an 80-year-old waitress who worked at Dinah's for more than three decades and was so beloved that she was often requested by regulars. There was also the famous wooden bar—kept intact since the fire—where customers carved their initials to mark their visit. Indeed, Dinah's is remembered fondly by many as a favorite Palo Alto institution that thrived for decades, eventually becoming a cultural smorgasbord of harps, fried chicken and Swedish delicacies.

But what to make of its disturbing symbols? While the restaurant may have begun as a fond tribute to a black woman and the food she cooked, under later owners and changing attitudes the slave imagery became troubling. By the 1950s, Dinah's Shack seemed to suggest an almost misty regard for the era of Southern slavery. While Dinah's mid-century white patrons seemed oblivious, today a restaurant theme of happy cooking slaves would be enough to start a picket line.

In the first half of the 20th century, however, such images were common. Dinah's mammy logo was reminiscent of the kindly slave and caregiver played by Hattie McDaniel in "Gone with the Wind" and prominent for decades on the labels of Aunt Jemima syrup. Mammies were usually fat and jolly and they became iconic symbols of the Jim Crow South. But the mammy character also symbolized a nefarious undertow in Southern society. As Dr. David Pilgrim, Professor of Sociology at Ferris State University, has written, "From slavery through the Jim Crow era, the mammy image served the political, social, and economic interests of mainstream white America. During slavery, the mammy caricature was posited as proof that blacks—in this case, black women—were contented, even happy, as slaves. Her wide grin, hearty laughter, and loyal servitude were offered as evidence of the supposed humanity of the institution of slavery."

By 1968, blacks were gaining political power and speaking out against blatantly racist symbols. Not surprisingly, the Palo Alto/Stanford branch of the NAACP went after Dinah's. The group called the restaurant's bandanna-capped mammy and stereotypically drawn stable boys "offensive," while a group of journalists in a Stanford fellowship program publicly boycotted the restaurant because of its "offensive racist symbols" and "perpetuation of stereotypes."

Responding to the criticism, Rickey does not seem to have really understood the objectionable meaning of the statues saying, "If they really feel it's necessary, we'll paint them white or make them Indians." In the end, Rickey opted for this "split the baby" approach, actually painting the stable boys white and lightening the overhead mammy sign, thereby eliciting a mocking response from the local papers. One letter to the editor read: "It is a sickly, stupid attempt to ignore history and by hiding the black faces, to atone for the blackness of our own hearts." Another: "Poor Dinah! Rest in Peace! Never again will I taste her 'Southern' fried chicken or her grand biscuits, as I cannot accept the hypocrisy of pink-cheeked stable boys." Today a few of the whitewashed statues still stand, having outlasted the restaurant itself.

Finally succumbing to the economics of earthquake retrofitting, Dinah's closed in 1989. Having long forgotten racial controversies, the local papers wrote tributes to the restaurant, recalling its glory days and vibrant history. Some recalled that original story behind the Dinah's Shack name. And perhaps in the end, having considered and noted the bitterness bred by caricatures of Dinah, we too should let our thoughts rest on the real Dinah and that day in 1926, when a white woman thought back to her youth and of her love for a black woman.

Three of the stable boy statues still stand on the old grounds now Trader Vic's restaurant. As you can see in the photo, their faces were literally painted white.
[PHOTO: BRIAN GEORGE]

John McQuarrie's mural depicts Leland Stanford surveying America's expansion into the West.

UNIVERSITY AVENUE TRAIN DEPOT
A Streamline to the Past

IN THE FINAL YEARS BEFORE THE GREAT MID-CENTURY DECLINE OF THE RAILROADS, PALO ALTO got itself a new train station. The Southern Pacific Railroad, still going strong in 1941 as a popular way to travel the country's western coast, decided to replace Palo Alto's aging depot with a sleek, modern station worthy of the city's hard-earned hub status. The new station was constructed in ultra-hip Streamline Moderne, a style that raced with the energy of a new age and looked toward the machines of the future. It turned out to be an ironic twist. For while the station's architecture spoke to modernity, the trains it served soon would become near relics of the past.

The base of University Avenue at Alma Street has long been a transportation center of Palo Alto. In the city's infancy, the first sheltered station—no more than a bench and overhanging roof really—was constructed on the Palo Alto side of the tracks for an auction sale of town lots. After being replaced by a larger enclosed structure, a new, yellow-tinged station was built on the Stanford side of the tracks with archways and some of the spectacle of the nearby university. As the local boarding point for the line to San Francisco, the new station served Stanford's 400 students and Palo Alto's 318 residents.

A large crowd of commuters await their train.

But this second edition was never particularly admired by locals. In a 1934 column, *Palo Alto Times* editor Dallas E. Wood criticized the station's "antiquity, architectural unloveliness and other deficiencies." And as early as the 1920s, his paper had been calling for a more "pretentious depot." Eventually, in conjunction with the construction of the University-Alma Street underpass, Southern Pacific announced plans for a new station for Palo Alto. On March 8, 1941, a grand parade of 2,000 people, 400 horses and a 40-by-75 foot flag marched down University Avenue to dedicate the new station.

As it happened, the blueprints for the station were laid out at the height of the Streamline Moderne architectural craze. Closely related to Art Deco, Streamline Moderne had a kind of "flash and gleam" beauty. Its look at the time—and remarkably, even six decades later—surged with progress and motion. As Professor David Gebhard has written, "Streamline Moderne offered a glimpse of the future. What it portended was a fully automated world in which machines, controlled by man, were everywhere invisible." With its dramatic rounded corners, narrow horizontal layering, glass brick windows and metal doors, Streamline Moderne conjured up a sense of movement and speed.

A train makes its way north from the old depot, 1894. The El Palo Alto tree is in the far distance along with the Palo Alto Hotel on Alma Street.

In some cases, Streamline Moderne buildings were actually constructed to resemble the purpose they served. For instance, the Palo Alto station was designed by Southern Pacific architect J.H. Christie to resemble a streamlined train while Palo Alto architect Birge Clark gave the local Sea Scout Building at the Baylands a rounded prow and porthole windows to suggest a ship. But as the style for a railroad station, Streamline Moderne actually pointed to a future that was moving away from rail travel. Streamline Moderne had an automobile-centered outlook that was often street or highway-oriented. And indeed, as the 1950s wore on, the popularity of passenger trains declined. A combination of the construction of the Eisenhower Administration's Interstate Highway System and a surge in commercial air travel left few Americans looking to ride the rails. By the 1960s, only legal obligations were keeping many passenger trains running and old streamliners such as the Daylight, Starlight, and Lark had become part of railroading history.

The old University Avenue depot in the 1930s, complete with shoeshine stand.

By 1970, the railroads accounted for seven percent of passenger travel in America. The following year, the major railroads were eaten up by Amtrak, a national railroad monopoly that has never been able to revitalize the intercity passenger train business. By the mid-1980s, operating losses led the Southern Pacific to sell the historic route between San Francisco and San Jose to a consortium of local transit authorities. Throughout these changes, the University Avenue station continued to serve commuters. These days the depot serves Caltrain, the commuter service that carries workers heading for the office towers of San Francisco and the office parks of Silicon Valley.

The station itself, however, remains much as it was in 1941 and now resides on the National Register of Historic Places. One of the few true Streamline Moderne buildings in the area, the 7,000-square-foot depot boasts a number of unique features, including an impressive 26-foot-long painting. John McQuarrie's grand—perhaps bordering on grandiose—mural depicts Leland Stanford surveying the progression of America's expansion into the West.

Renovation projects in 1981 and 2000 restored the station's classic seating and lighting while expanding its functionality. It now serves as a transportation hub for buses, shuttles and even bicycle rental. Recently an upscale cafe set up shop in the depot to serve thirsty commuters.

Today the University Avenue depot still stands near the spot where the first train station stood before the city itself existed. And as such, it remains witness to both an architectural style that looked forward and a railroading history rooted in our past.

The new station.

The new Palo Alto Animal Shelter as seen in 1937.

THE HUMANE SOCIETY
A History of Compassion

There was a time when the life of a city animal was a lot less domesticated than it is today. Before the advent of leash laws, license tags, pooper scoopers and pet daycare, city life for dogs and cats ran a little closer to the wild side. Without these laws, our four-legged friends enjoyed an independence that allowed them to roam the neighborhoods and seek out adventure. Today, some longtime pet lovers may still have fond memories for those old neighborhood dogs waiting for their young masters outside the school each day or chasing down speeding cars. But of course, with such adventures also came the danger and potential cruelties of a life not so sheltered by an owner with leash in hand. Luckily, in early day Palo Alto there was a group of concerned citizens always looking out for the city's furry friends.

In 2008, the Palo Alto Humane Society celebrated its 100th birthday as protector of Palo Alto's animal population. This nonprofit group has been responsible through the years for such tasks as running the city pound, treating hurt and stray animals, monitoring the conditions of farm animals and preventing animal cruelty. It has been said that a society is ultimately judged by how it treats its weakest, most vulnerable members. If so, then Palo Alto owes a debt of gratitude for the 100 years of service that the PAHS has advocated for the city's animal voiceless and vulnerable.

The Palo Alto Humane Society's long history dates back to old Mrs. B. C. Merriman, who as legend has it once rode the Palo Alto streets whip in hand, ready to teach a lesson to any driver she saw mistreating his horse. In 1902, the founding members of the Society's predecessor Palo Alto SPCA included Stanford's first president David Starr Jordan and Jane Stanford herself, both of whom helped push for the city's first horse watering trough in the days before automobiles. In 1908, the Society renamed itself to become the Palo Alto Humane Society (PAHS).

Poundmaster Gerald Dalmadge makes a new friend in 1950.

Two dogs seen in the cages of the old animal shelter.

But it wasn't really until 1924 that the PAHS found its voice. Police Chief C. F. Noble ordered a crackdown on unlicensed dogs roaming the streets. Playing the villain to a tee, Noble hired a man called Dick the Dogcatcher to enforce justice. Soon the papers were full of letters from readers complaining about maimed dogs that were swiped from their home yards and porches. There was also a history of the police operating with a "shoot on sight" policy for strays.

Clearly, there was a need for the Humane Society to help safeguard the city's pets and strays from this rather overzealous police force. But the PAHS had little money and no land. Enter Mrs. Frank Thomas (as she was called in the papers of the day), a Middlefield Road resident who was known for taking in as many stray pets as her home and husband would allow. Before long, the PAHS had set up kennels in her yard and acquired her services to care for animals being rounded up all over the city. Finally, two years later, the city spent $2,000 to build a makeshift pound.

A decade later, the PAHS was able to finally build a first-rate shelter thanks in part to $11,000 donated by Mrs. Marguerite Ravenscroft of Santa Barbara. The new quarters, built in 1937 at the current location of El Camino's Sheraton Hotel, were described by the *Palo Alto Times* in 1947 as an "animal utopia," complete with air-conditioning, heating and beds for some 50 dogs and 25 cats. The shelter included full kitchen service for animal meal preparation, one-way receiving kennels where lost animals could be dropped off after hours and a tub for bathing dogs.

Indeed, contemporary newspaper accounts tell of a happy animal atmosphere full of characters such as Trigger, a quick and feisty feline who after catching her daily allotment of mice and rats would head out to the parking lot to clear out the gophers. Moving at a slower pace was Ol' Pa, a desert turtle who promenaded along the kennel fence torturing the yelping puppies below.

But the shelter took care of more than just dogs, cats and the occasional turtle. Monkeys, raccoons, porcupines, ducks, turtles and skunks all found their way onto the roster—not to mention a rare visit from a wolf or a crocodile. The shelter also employed an ambulance service for sick and injured animals around town. During World War II, the Society used its vehicles to save dozens of animals that Japanese-Americans were forced to leave behind during their internment in war relocation camps authorized by U.S. Executive Order 9066.

Education has always been an important tenet of the Palo Alto Humane Society's mission. In its early days, the PAHS visited schools to teach children the proper way to treat animals—even organizing "Bands of Mercy" to encourage children to keep an eye out for local animals in need.

But when educating the community was not enough, the Society was not afraid to use legal action to protect animals in Palo Alto. For instance, the PAHS's annual report from 1939 details how five offenders were taken before judges that year after failing to heed the Humane Society's warnings for improperly chaining their dogs. In 1984, the PAHS brought a lawsuit against Stanford University and the Veterans Administration for abuse in the care of a white Samoyed dog named Snowball who was found in pain with open wounds and incisions.

When legal action was not possible, the Society sometimes found other ways to help animals in need. In one case, the PAHS purchased a blind horse to take it out of the "horse-trading racket," putting it out to pasture with other older horses at Mrs. Frances Newhall Wood's appropriately-named Hawthorne Happy Home for Horses. Other times the Society's work took them off the Peninsula. During the terrible Sacramento River floods of 1940, PAHS officers travelled more than 21,000 miles to rescue stray, sick and abandoned animals.

During the 1960s, the Humane Society responded to the times by becoming more involved in political issues. For instance, in 1961 PAHS President Gerald Dalmadge took a firm stand against Stanford University School of Medicine's desire to use the shelter's unclaimed animals for research. Citing the agreement with which Mrs. Ravenscroft had given $11,000 to help built the shelter in 1937, Dalmadge said that it would be a "violation of the principles under which the shelter was established." Eventually Stanford withdrew its request, citing "strong public reaction."

In 1972 the Humane Society ceded control of the shelter to the city. Since then, the PAHS remains heavily involved in advocacy and education: "Instead of managing animals inside a shelter, we work to keep animals out of the shelter." It neuters 1,000 homeless animals and pets annually, provides emergency rescue care, maintains a hotline and is designing an elementary curriculum for California schools. In the past two decades, the PAHS has flexed political muscle by rallying against greyhound racing, steel jaw leghold traps and decompression chambers for euthanizing shelter animals. PAHS has also launched Humane Planet, a program to promote humane dining options and certify restaurants and caterers that meet specific standards.

In 2008, the PAHS fought hard for Proposition 2, a state ballot initiative that sought to eliminate the cruel confinement of California farm animals. Indeed, the passage of Prop 2 demonstrates that while Dick the Dogcatcher may be long gone, there is still much to do as the Palo Alto Humane Society heads into its second century.

These concrete holding pens held animals left at the shelter when the shelter was closed.

The yard of the old animal shelter.

An aerial view of the Varian building on Hansen Way under construction. A portion of Barron Park is visible at the bottom of the photo and El Camino Real can be seen at the upper right.

STANFORD RESEARCH PARK
The Engine of Silicon Valley

Y OU DON'T HEAR ABOUT THE EASTERN ESTABLISHMENT SO MUCH ANYMORE. BUT THERE was a time when to be taken seriously in business, politics and most other fields, you pretty much had to be a product of the East. It seemed that all the power players, big money men and members of the Old Boys' Club went to Harvard, Yale or one of the other East Coast powerhouses. California just wasn't the big leagues. Maybe it was because the Golden State was the home for Hollywood romances or because the weather was more suitable for the Beach Boys than bigwigs in three-piece suits—but for whatever reason, California had trouble getting its due respect. And this could be rather frustrating for a school with a growing reputation like Stanford University. While being called the "Harvard of the West" certainly earned Stanford some respect in the postwar years, it still had to settle for a kind of second-class citizenship.

This bothered Stanford engineering professor Frederick Terman. After all, even his protégés Bill Hewlett and David Packard headed out east to MIT and General Electric after studying at Stanford. "In those days," Terman would later say, "a serious young engineer had to go back east to put spit and polish on his education." Unsatisfied with this arrangement, Terman began to consider how Stanford might further a kind of western intellectual center that could rival the eminence of eastern hotspots. He envisioned a collaboration between academia and industry that would benefit both, and—thanks to Stanford's land and interest—Terman actually made it happen. During the 1950s, Frederick Terman played the pivotal role in encouraging the entrepreneurial partnerships with Stanford University that set off a world-famous techie boom. The innovative center was called the Stanford Industrial Park, and it would become the heartbeat of what came to be known as Silicon Valley.

Frederick Terman, the "Father of Silicon Valley"

An early image of the famous HP garage at 367 Addison Avenue. [HEWLETT-PACKARD COMPANY]

Frederick Terman was only at Stanford because he got sick. Although he grew up on the campus—his father Lewis was the Stanford psychology professor who invented the IQ test—Terman had earned his doctorate at MIT and was expecting to return to Cambridge as an assistant professor when he came down with tuberculosis while summer vacationing back home. Two doctors declared his case hopeless as he spent the next year with sandbags on his stomach, playing with ham radios and drafting his first book on radio engineering. In 1925, as Terman's condition gradually improved, he was offered a half-time teaching job at Stanford. Getting out of bed for just the two hours a day it took to go to class, Terman began to rise through the ranks of academia as his health also advanced.

Terman's career at Stanford was remarkable. In his early days at the university he made the electrical department one of the best in the nation. An avid inventor, Terman filed 36 patents between 1930 and 1947 and was elected president of the Institute of Radio Engineers in 1940—the first person west of Pittsburgh to achieve the honor. During World War II he went east to direct a staff of more than 850 at the Radio Research Laboratory at Harvard University, which had the crucial responsibility for developing the jammers and aluminum chaff used to confuse enemy radar. Earlier, of course, he had lured Bill and Dave back to Palo Alto and helped them get what would become a billion dollar company off the ground. Still, it was his work in establishing the Stanford Industrial Park that would make him the "Father of Silicon Valley."

Of course, while Terman may have seen the Stanford Industrial Park as a means to rival the Eastern Establishment in electronics, the university itself actually needed the money. After a postwar downturn in its endowment fund, Stanford was looking for a way to make some extra cash. While Leland Stanford's will precluded the university from selling off its great excesses of land, there was no reason it could not be leased to interested parties. So under the direction of financially savvy business manager Alf Brandin, Stanford began to pursue two profitable projects—a shopping center on land to the north of the university and a park for light industry to the south.

Still, it would take the influence of Frederick Terman to make the Stanford Industrial Park a place to be. Calling the park "our secret weapon," Terman began to convince companies to come to Palo Alto and set up shop at what would be the first university-owned industrial park in the world. First aboard was Varian Associates, a growing company with ties to Terman and Stanford, which obtained a park lease in 1951. Terman then convinced Hewlett-Packard to head out to Page Mill Road, where its headquarters remain to this day. Soon a flood of other corporations would make Stanford Industrial Park one of the most respected addresses on the West Coast—and eventually give the Peninsula a collection of big name companies to rival any conglomeration back east. General Electric, Eastman Kodak and Lockheed were among dozens of others that joined Varian and HP, transforming the old Valley of Heart's Delight into the ultramodern Silicon Valley.

A name change in the 1970s to Stanford Research Park underlined the focus of cooperation between the university and the tech companies. From Xerox PARC came innovations that led to the PC explosion of the 1980s and the dot-com boom and bubble of the 1990s. The bust that followed hit the Valley hard but today Terman's vision of academic and business co-partnership still thrives and an address in Stanford Research Park still looks pretty good on a business card. Looking back on his creation in his declining years, Frederick Terman reflected, "When we set out to create a community of technical scholars in Silicon Valley, there wasn't much here and the rest of the world looked awfully big. Now a lot of the rest of the world is here." And of course, that includes most of those big boys from back east.

Russell and Sigurd Varian, the brothers were the park's first tenants. [VARIAN ASSOCIATES]

An overhead shot of the Stanford Shopping Center in the 1960s. The Macy's store is apparent at center left and the Emporium at center right. Parking lots surround the mall in these days before the parking structures were built.

STANFORD SHOPPING CENTER
Turning Pastures into Profits

IN MANY WAYS PALO ALTO'S STANFORD SHOPPING CENTER REPRESENTS THE TYPICAL American mall. Built in the early days of the great suburban migration, the new shopping plaza north of Stanford immediately drew shoppers away from the traditional downtown Palo Alto commercial district. And yet Stanford Shopping Center has never been completely typical. Founded as a special source of income for Stanford University, its beginnings certainly were unique. Furthermore, as an open-air center which has grown in stages and also undergone a dramatic upscale shift over the years, the Stanford Shopping Center has never been easily classified. These days it hardly resembles the typical multi-tiered, air-conditioned "box with food court" that has become the prototypical American mall. As Palo Alto has become the capital of Silicon Valley's success, the Stanford Shopping Center has grown to accommodate the new wealth that has flooded the city. Long gone are Palo Alto's days as a sleepy small town—and long gone are the days of the Stanford Shopping Center as a sleepy small-town mall.

Cars race along El Camino Real past the future location of the Stanford Shopping Center.

The Stanford Shopping Center began as an ingenious way for the financially strapped Stanford University of the early 1950s to make money on the side. In 1947, business manager Alf Brandin began pushing a plan to cash in on Stanford's abundance of undeveloped land through the construction of a mall—the profits from which would go directly to the university's general fund.

A shopping mall in Palo Alto did make economic sense. Consumer studies done at the time demonstrated that thousands of locals weathered the hour-long train ride to San Francisco to spend nearly $200 million annually at department stores in Union Square and around the big city. Put some of those San Francisco stores down in Palo Alto, Brandin figured, and locals would simply motor over to park and shop right in their own hometown.

Alf Brandin, center, business manager and executive officer for land development for Stanford University, seated with a committee studying a map. Architectural diagrams and drawings are on the wall behind them.

A '50s era photo showing the Emporium and Roos Bros. flanking the entrance to Stanford Shopping Center.

Although an outside firm recommended that the center be built on the auto row area of Menlo Park along El Camino, the university eventually settled on developing the 62 acres they owned further south on the King's Highway just within the Palo Alto border. In 1953, the first rumblings of construction began in those hayfields and by 1956 the $15 million Stanford Shopping Center was open for business. Stanford was now the nation's first university to buffer its own endowment pool by building itself a mall.

By comparison to what the Stanford Shopping Center has become, this initial effort was modest—maybe even a bit homespun. These were the early days of the American mall, when shopping was still seen as more business than pleasure. While the present-day Stanford Shopping Center has stores offering to dress your baby fashionably, put an adorable sweater on your pet or sell you the perfect recliner designed for a first grader, the original mall was a little more meat and potatoes. The 1956 center included Purity Market, Woolworth's, Donnelley's Hardware Store, a thrift store, a shoe repair shop—and literal meat and potatoes at Eat-Rite restaurant. And as Alf Brandin had hoped, the new mall also lured some of San Francisco's prestigious stores down the Peninsula, among them the Emporium, Sommer & Kaufman Shoes and I. Magnin & Co.

Still, despite a number of stores that would be at home on any Main Street USA, the new shopping center was tough on Palo Alto's own main street. Many of the downtown stores rushed to set up shop at the new mall—some even choosing to close their long-standing University Avenue locations. Roos Bros., for example, settled into their modern 17,000 square-foot Stanford Shopping Center location in 1956 just as they let their downtown lease expire.

Of course, it's not as if downtown merchants didn't see it coming. In fact, after plans were announced in 1952 that Stanford would be turning their pastures into profits, Hillsdale Shopping Center builder David Bohannan proposed a massive overhaul of downtown Palo Alto to rival the coming economic threat. His plan to replace most of the buildings between Alma and Cowper along University Avenue with "an even larger shopping center in the heart of downtown" symbolized a widespread loss of faith in the American city. As Bohannan said, "such developments are going to save many cities and fill the needs of our society." In reality, his plan would pretty much have flattened downtown in favor of five large department stores and a half dozen double-decked parking lots—requiring the razing of every building in a 50-acre area. Thankfully, the momentum for this nuclear option died down once Stanford Shopping Center opened for business.

Still, there was no doubt that for more than three decades, downtown was hurt by the competition. As repeated in scores of American cities in the 1960s and '70s, Palo Alto's downtown could not compete with the convenience of a suburban shopping center. By the 1970s empty storefronts increasingly made University Avenue a ghost town. And Stanford Shopping Center managers were not exactly resting on their laurels. Newer and more illustrious department stores opened—Macy's in 1961, Saks in 1963, Bullock's (later Nordstrom) in 1972 and Neiman Marcus in 1985.

Additionally, Stanford's hiring of Rosemary McAndrews to direct the center in the early 1970s signaled a move toward a more high-end shopping experience. In 1976, the Palo Alto City Council approved an enormous expansion of the center that allowed McAndrews to go to town. Policy changes forced many stores into smaller quarters and some larger leases were bought out. McAndrews and her team then took to fashioning the old mall into a sort of European street fair. Using photos of markets and shopping plazas taken while on trips to the Old World, McAndrews made what was once a good place to buy a new lawnmower, ladder or shirt into the place to purchase a trendy Italian sports coat or rare oriental fragrance. The center's appearance changed dramatically as well, with the addition of lush gardens, fanciful sculptures and a grand mural of a European market rather self-consciously named the "Rue du Chat qui Peche" after a famous Parisian alley. By 1985, the Euro strategy had paid off, quite literally, as its 150 stores led the Peninsula with annual earnings of $250 million.

Rosemary McAndrews brought a new kind of class to the old mall.

In the 1990s, the shopping center took yet another step into retail swank when the Emporium was replaced by the first Bloomingdale's to open west of the Rockies. Its "Ultimate Premiere" in November 1996 featured a sold-out concert with Liza Minnelli singing at a tent party catered by Paula LeDuc—and an entrance fee running between $250 and $1,000. Since 2003, professional mallers Simon Property Group has owned and managed the center under a long-term lease. Though these days the university is no longer directing operations at Stanford Shopping Center, you are still invited to breakfast at Tiffany's, eat French bread at La Baguette or tempt your sweet tooth at Teuscher Chocolates of Switzerland.

But is Palo Alto becoming the Beverly Hills of the north? In this new millennium, University Avenue has bounced back largely by imitating Stanford Shopping Center's appeal to higher tax brackets. Even as the financial crisis that emerged in 2008 continues to depress local business, the question lingers whether Palo Altans will be permanently priced out of their own hometown.

Duncan and Mercedes Williams on his final day as manager of the Winter Club.

THE WINTER LODGE
Skating Through the Political Process

Young skaters enjoy the Winter Lodge ambiance in this recent photo. [WINTER LODGE]

IT HAS BEEN SAID THAT DEMOCRACY IS A PARTICIPATORY SPORT. AND INDEED IN AMERICA only the citizens and communities that can effectively lobby their elected officials tend to get what they want. Contrary to popular opinion, politicians do listen to their constituents. After all, any time phone calls to Congressional offices are running 10–1 against a controversial bill, you can bet its political viability will be short-lived. It's also true that virtually every urban blight-causing, cross-city highway has wound up in the wards of the poor and politically unorganized.

So it is possible to fight city hall, but you've got to have the time, money and stamina to attend council meetings, collect signatures, stand on street corners, and wear down the system. Of course, in Palo Alto, citizens can be pretty persistent in that wearing-down process. And that's one reason that Palo Alto remains the kind of city where you want to raise your kids. They play the sport of democracy pretty well here—and it shows.

Case in point: that once-doomed local institution known today as the Winter Lodge. In 1981, it was announced that the only permanent outdoor ice skating rink west of the Sierra Nevada was scheduled to close at the end of the 1983 winter skating season. In response, local ice skating enthusiasts waged an epic battle, overcoming wads of red tape and eventually proving that intense political participation can pay off.

Ice skating in Palo Alto began in 1956, thanks to San Jose State engineering professor Duncan Williams. After migrating to Palo Alto from chilly Wisconsin, Williams experimented with how to freeze an ice skating rink in milder weather. Using a refrigerant system with a brine solution in the pipes and some strategically placed shade, Williams managed to create a functional outdoor rink in Palo Alto's less-than-freezing winter. But while his engineering skills proved successful, it

Figure skater Alan Bell practicing at the Winter Club, 1980s.

was unclear whether his marketing strategy was particularly honed. As Williams would later say, "it was sort of a wild adventure. I didn't have very good grounds to know it would [succeed]."

On February 15th, 1956, The Winter Club opened in an undeveloped area along Middlefield Road. It was an immediate hit. California ice was a skate down memory lane for the many non-native Palo Altans who had spent their childhood winters twirling triple salchows or falling on their backsides at rinks back east. For California kids, lacing up winter skates had a novelty appeal—and offered a little taste of what they were missing in a nearly single-climate region.

The Winter Club consisted of an outdoor rink—compact at 65 by 125 feet—as well as a separate smaller area for "patch practicing" figure skaters. It operated on individual and family memberships, and by 1959 the rink was running at a 500-family peak capacity. The Winter Club hosted youth hockey, junior ice follies and birthday parties as well as open skate nights. Throughout the '60s and '70s, Williams turned a consistent profit in the warm California sun.

By 1981, however, the Winter Club's driving force was finally hanging up his skates. Williams planned to retire in 1983, at the end of his lease, while owner Richard Peery intended to knock down the rink and put up condos. A small group of ice skating *aficionados* entered the fray. Determined to keep ice skating in Palo Alto, they proposed either renovating the rink or building a new one. The pro-skating movement began with the establishment in 1981 of the non-profit Friends of the Winter Club. Their initial pitch was to build a new rink at half-completed Greer Park, but a rather confrontational meeting with 40 or so West Bayshore residents scuttled that plan.

Regrouping, the Friends of the Winter Club found another city-owned parcel—technically park land—just west of the Palo Alto Golf Course near Geng Road. After getting a favorable lease option from the City Council, the skaters were soon making plans to build a grand 250 by 150 foot outdoor ice rink—dubbed the Friendship Pavilion. It would serve as an ice skating rink in the colder months and host dance, music and gymnastics in the summertime.

But the group found it could not raise enough money in private donations to build the pavilion. Back at the drawing board, the Friends asked the Palo Alto City Council to put up a loan to build it. The city balked at that idea. Then, scrapping all hopes for a new ice rink, the group entertained the possibility of renovating the closing Winter Club. Back to the council they went to request $175,000 to make "crucial repairs" to the Middlefield site. Again the council said no.

But Palo Altans are a tenacious group. As the day of reckoning approached in April of 1983, the pro-skating forces reorganized under the leadership of future Palo Alto councilman Jack Morton as the Trust for Community Skating. Seeking the help of the YMCA to run the rink, and appealing to better angels, the Trust convinced landowner Peery to give them a one-year lease extension. They even successfully lobbied the City Council to pony up $25,000 for repairs. In September of 1983, the rink opened for the first time in 27 years without Duncan Williams. It was largely unchanged except for a new name—The Winter Lodge.

Still, skating in Palo Alto remained on thin ice. As the end of the 1984 season rolled around, the Trust for Community Skating was still desperately searching for the $2.5 million needed to purchase the Lodge from Peery. Again the skaters went into City Hall looking for a loan, and again they came out empty-handed. So the Trust decided to circumvent the council with an appeal to the public; the Trust collected signatures to put a measure on the fall ballot requiring the city to "provide, fund and maintain an ice skating facility." Passage of the initiative seemed unlikely, though, once the idea was lambasted in the local press as being overly directive.

Meanwhile, as the 1985 election approached, the skaters came up with a better idea. In an inspired bit of real estate creativity, the Trust cooked up a plan in which the city would swap the land at Geng Road for Peery's Winter Lodge plot. Peery would get to develop his new land while the Winter Lodge could stay in place. Everyone would be a winner. Only you don't just go around swapping city land like baseball cards. Lawyers deduced that not one, but two, ballot initiatives would need voter approval in order to legalize the scheme. One initiative was necessary to allow the city to make such a trade at all, while another authorized the Geng Road parcel for non-park use. Finally, in November 1985, the voters overwhelmingly approved both Measures A and B. A few more years went by before the swap was consummated, but in the end the Trust had found a way to keep skating in Palo Alto.

Today the Winter Lodge has one of the largest skating schools in the country, enrolling over 3,000 skating students per season, and in 2007 it ranked as one of the top 10 outdoor ice skating experiences in the country. The Winter Lodge remains one of Palo Alto's gems, an enduring attraction with an unlikely story. But while the glistening ice and evergreen trees create a sense of timelessness, the truth is that its existence is the result of some very timely political grunt work.

Young skaters enjoy the ice in this photo from the Winter Club era.

Josina Bol and her donkey, Mickey, 1986.

THE BOL PARK DONKEYS
Neighborhood Pets

Barron Park, the southwest section of Palo Alto, has always had a rustic, pastoral feel. It was not incorporated into the city of Palo Alto until 1975 (despite the kicking and screaming of some residents) and much of the area still lacks sidewalks and gutters. Located west of bustling El Camino Real, a trip to Barron Park can seem like a step back in time. The back roads of the neighborhood pass by tall redwoods, babbling creeks and overgrown bushes. Although Silicon Valley has boomed around it, Barron Park has been able to keep much of its old-time character.

But certainly no image of the neighborhood could attest to Barron Park's countrified flavor like the sight of a man jogging through Bol Park with a donkey on leash. That would be Pericles (Perry to close friends), one of two donkeys who live at Bol Park and serve as would-be neighborhood mascots.

From 1962 to 1972, the donkeys lived in the pasture that became Bol Park, surrounded by apricot orchards and strawberry fields. It was then the property of one Cornelis Bol, a long-time Stanford researcher and inventor of the mercury vapor light who moved to Palo Alto from his native Holland to escape the Nazis. Bol often allowed the neighborhood kids to play with—and even ride—the donkeys that grazed the pasture in the 1960s. And if a group of donkeys wandered away and began marching around the neighborhood in single file—as they were apt to do—local kids rounded them up and led them back to pasture. Since 1972, they have lived in the current donkey pasture on private land. It seems the donkeys have always been seen as community pets.

In fact, in the 1960s, the most beloved of the donkeys—a distinctive black donkey named Negrita—had the pleasure of serving as the Gunn High School mascot at football games. Later

Cornelis Bol, Stanford professor and inventor of the mercury vapor light, at work in his study.

Paul Wolff (on left) and Richard Placone pose with Negrita the donkey in Bol Park in 1969.

The author standing with Barron Park's resident donkey, Perry, the model for Donkey in the movie, "Shrek." [PHOTO: MATT BOWLING]

it was Mickey who became a Barron Park favorite even though he was known as the "braying-est donkey this side of the Holy Land," according to Barron Park historian Doug Graham.

The destiny of the pasture and the donkeys became closely tied. After Cornelis Bol died in 1965, the neighborhood mobilized to fulfill Bols' wish that the land become a neighborhood park. After residents taxed themselves, lobbied successfully for federal matching grants, and constructed a pedestrian path, play structure and other amenities, Bol Park officially opened in April of 1974.

When Mrs. Bol died in 1996, some worried about Mickey's fate. But in the spirit of the Barron Park community, he was adopted by neighborhood volunteers. Later he was joined by Perry, a miniature equine and Niner, a former Mojave Desert resident with a keen ability to open gate latches. Although Mickey died in 1998, his friends live on today in Bol Park, aided by half a dozen volunteers who feed, walk and care for the donkeys. All donkey expenses—more than a $1,000 a year—are paid through voluntary donations.

Sunday mornings, the donkeys are the center of attention during their famed park strolls. The donkeys make friends easily, both with local dogs and children. And the Sunday promenades give the equines a chance to nibble on Bol Park's lush green grass while the kids get to pet and stroke the donkeys. Volunteers teach donkey safety and handling.

But perhaps you feel like you've seen Perry before? You probably have. In the early '90s, the then Palo Alto-based Pacific Data Images (which later merged with Dreamworks) stopped by Bol Park and took more than 100 images of Perry to serve as the model for the famed sidekick Donkey in "Shrek." Although, the company donated $75 for Perry's participation, he received no mention in the credits—a fact that still rankles some of his handlers. But supposedly, Perry's somewhat edgy personality did make it to the big screen. Hang out with Perry, the handlers say, and you'll see Donkey's disposition first-hand. It is unknown whether Eddie Murphy and Perry ever met to confer on the role.

LONG AGO

Looking down University Avenue from the Circle after the 1906 quake.

THE 1906 EARTHQUAKE
"Like a Terrier Shaking a Rat"

PALO ALTO WAS STILL A VERY YOUNG CITY WHEN IT FACED ITS GREATEST CRISIS—THE earthquake of 1906. While San Francisco and Stanford University suffered more damage, the effect on Palo Alto was severe and extensive. It would prove to be a kind of coming-of-age moment for the new city—the first big test. As it turned out, Palo Altans rallied and immediately vowed to rebuild. Town boosters even saw an opportunity to seize the moment and entice residents fleeing from San Francisco to settle in Palo Alto. While that plan had little success, it is clear that the 1906 earthquake did not wreck the city, but rather revitalized it.

At 5:12 on the morning of April 18, 1906, the earth moved along the San Andreas Fault, and Palo Alto and the Bay Area were rocked by a 47-second, 8.3 magnitude earthquake. Most residents awoke in their beds to the terror of trembling floors and falling chimneys. Merchant C. H. Christensen wrote to a cousin in Chicago, "I was lying in bed, half asleep, when I heard a roar in the distance, and before I could get up, the house began to shake with that sinking motion peculiar to earthquakes, and then there came a twisting lurch which did the damage." Palo Alto resident and Stanford Professor Guido Marx recalled being "rudely awakened by the shaking of the house and the accompanying rumble, roar and crash. 'What is it?' said [my wife]. 'It's an earthquake and a bad one,' I replied… I felt nothing could survive such vicious shaking, that this was the end for us. It was like a terrier shaking a rat." While over at Stanford, Dr. Olaf P. Jenkins remembered that "Since my bed was walking all over my bedroom and I was sure that the house would land on its side, I just hung on."

In less than a minute, half the chimneys in Palo Alto had fallen to the ground and nearly every business in town had been damaged. A few buildings completely collapsed, including

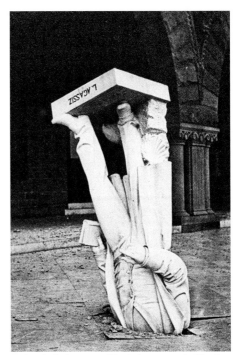

At Stanford, the statue of Louis Agassiz crashed head-first to the ground below.

Inside Memorial Church at Stanford University following the earthquake. [PILLSBURY PICTURE CO.]

F. C. Thiele's new $30,000 store and Fuller's High Street grocery. The four-year-old Simkins Building lost its first-floor walls, while the two top stories were reported by local papers to be "some three feet out of plumb." Things weren't much better at Frazer & Company's Stanford Building, where the walls fell to the ground leaving sleepers unexpectedly exposed to the elements. Fraternal Hall at 140 University lost its cornice and second-story wall, which crashed into Crandall's Bicycle Shop below. The final bill for Palo Alto's cleanup totaled more than $165,000 in 1906 dollars.

Over at Stanford the damage was worse. Perhaps most symbolically, a statue of geologist Louis Agassiz was knocked off its pedestal and crashed head first into the pavement below. But the devastation was more than just symbolic. The façade of the Memorial Church was shattered when its towering spire fell into the nave, the newly completed Stanford Library was utterly devastated, the gymnasium was ruined and the Memorial Arch cracked and had to be demolished. Reconstruction costs at the university eventually added up to more than $2.8 million.

Two men died in the Stanford wreckage. Sophomore Junius Hannah was hit by a falling chimney at Encina Hall, and a young fireman, Otto Gerdes, was killed when the 110 foot power house chimney collapsed after he raced to the boiler room and heroically shut off campus power.

Palo Alto avoided the catastrophic fires of San Francisco, thanks in part to engineer Robert McGlynn, who was at the Palo Alto power plant when the quake hit. Seeing the 60 foot tower dangerously swaying above him, he had the presence of mind to immediately cut off the town's power supply, helping assure Palo Alto of water and electricity in the days to come.

But along with such heroics, there was panicky behavior as well. Some Palo Altans raided stores seeking groceries, fearing that they would soon be cut off from San Francisco supplies. Meanwhile at Stanford, an athlete with a loaded pistol reportedly stood on guard protecting female students from "potential rapists," while armed guards on watch at Palo Alto bridges defended the city from "undesirables and potential burglars."

As Palo Altans began to right their own lives, their thoughts turned to what was happening to the north. On the evening of the quake, the *Palo Alto Times* managed—rather determinedly—to get out the paper's first ever "Extra" by using a hand press and old pied type cases. Its headline spurred action: "San Francisco's Dead Estimated at 1,500; Stricken City in Flames." The grim portrait soon led to frenzied preparation, as Palo Altans readied themselves for the onslaught of refugees that seemed destined to come their way—estimates on the day following the quake ran as high as 6,000. This expectation was fueled by the rather remarkable claim that Palo Altans could actually read newspapers from the light of San Francisco fires on the horizon and hear the dynamiting of buildings.

Only about 550 San Franciscans actually took refuge in Palo Alto—but there were enough that the *San Jose Mercury* could refer to the city three days after the earthquake as "one grand haven of rest for the sick, homeless and needy earthquake and fire sufferers from San Francisco." Still, the paper pointed out that "the chief disappointment [Palo Altans] have seems to be that so few sufferers are coming to [their] doors."

The evening after the earthquake hit, the Palo Alto and Stanford Relief Committee organized at the Circle (near the present day University Avenue underpass). Palo Alto women served 250 to 300 meals each day at the Congregational Church and sewed badly needed baby outfits. And when it was discovered that damaged rail lines and injuries were preventing many San Franciscans from heading south, volunteers went to the big city, eventually bringing 75,000 loaves of bread, 10,000 gallons of milk and 1,200 sacks of clothing, as well as other badly needed supplies.

Palo Alto also remained steady in its determination to rebuild following the earthquake. One headline in the *Palo Alto Daily Times* days after the quake announced "Faith in Palo Alto Unshaken." The article told of the large sign that had been mounted at the corner of University and Ramona announcing, "A modern building for the First National Bank will be erected on this corner. The earthquake has not impaired our capital nor shaken our confidence in the growth of Palo Alto." Meanwhile, Board of Trustees President J. F. Parkinson received great cheers from a Relief Committee audience when he told them, "If I had a dollar tonight, I would invest it in Palo Alto real estate and rest assured that I had acted wisely." Just two weeks after the earthquake struck, the *Palo Alto Tribune* told of "work of construction and reconstruction rapidly going forward." The majority of merchants were back to business as usual within a fortnight.

There were even some town fathers who envisioned the quake as a chance for Palo Alto to achieve some considerable growth. "We will never again get such a chance to boom our town," Trade Board President Marshall Black declared. Hoping to attract San Francisco residents who might still work in the city but would be looking for homes elsewhere, Palo Alto advertised itself as the perfect commuter suburb. The J. J. Morris Real Estate Company tried to entice potential

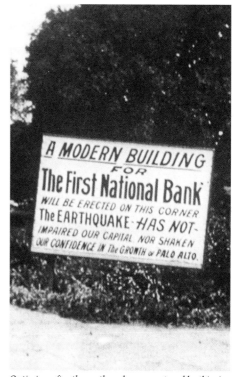

Optimism after the earthquake was captured by this sign.

residents by offering "beautiful cottage homes," at $25 per month and declaring that "This is Palo Alto's opportunity… The tide of residence travel will turn across the bay and down the Peninsula."

These efforts were somewhat compromised, however, by a dispute between the city and F. C. Thiele, the owner of a fallen building that stood in ruins just across the tracks from the University

The F. C. Thiele Building on Alma Street was an eyesore and publicity problem for Palo Alto following the earthquake.

Avenue Southern Pacific train station. This disquieting visage led many out-of-town travelers to believe that Palo Alto had fared much worse than it had during the earthquake—a perception problem that eventually prompted city officials to take matters into their own hands. On June 4th, with the building still in shambles, the city ordered workers to clear the debris on the street and throw it back onto the Thiele property at "the owner's expense." The Palo Alto Promotion Committee was even planning to erect a large signboard blocking the unsightly building from the view of commuters, when the wreckage was finally cleared up by the owner.

In the end, Palo Alto did not become a booming commuter town following the earthquake, but its real estate market did rebound nicely, business boomed again and the small town survived that first big test. For sure, the 1906 earthquake had shaken Palo Alto, but it had also stirred resilience and a sense of community pride.

Above: the corner of Emerson and University shown 2008. [PHOTO: MATT BOWLING]

Left: the same corner shown after the 1906 quake. Frazer's Dry Goods Store suffered severe damage; the second floor walls basically fell into the street, leaving the apartments above without any siding.

Palo Alto Fire Department Volunteers pulling a hose cart in a race held in Hollister, 1904.

PALO ALTO'S EARLY FIRES
Fearing the Flames

IN THE LATE 19TH AND EARLY 20TH CENTURY, EVERY CITY DWELLER HAD TO FEAR FIRE. Fire caused more urban destruction in the decade after the Civil War than the war itself. No city—big or small—was safe from a fire disaster. In 1871, flames swept across Chicago, burning four square miles of the city and killing hundreds. Boston burned the following year, when a fire originating in the basement of a downtown warehouse led to a 12-hour inferno that consumed 776 buildings. And years later, things hadn't gotten a whole lot better. Baltimore went down in 1901 and much of San Francisco was lost in the fires that were touched off by the 1906 earthquake.

Of course, in those days cities were essentially large collections of kindling ready to ignite at the smallest spark. Wooden houses were erected with wooden roofs—all on top of explosive gas lines leading to manually lit street lamps. Inside houses, candles and gas lamps were always a stray arm away from setting off an uncontrollable blaze. Small towns usually had either volunteer fire departments or no organized fire fighters at all. In addition, the many fully or over-insured buildings gave developers little incentive to design fire-safe structures.

In a small town like Palo Alto, every house and building was in jeopardy. Indeed, newspapers from the city's first few decades contain almost weekly reports of local conflagrations.

In the 1890s, before the establishment of the town's volunteer fire department, homes and businesses stood little chance of surviving fires. The *Palo Alto Times* of August 2, 1895, reported the burning of Mrs. A. J. Harper's residence on High Street. Onlookers had already crowded around the house when flames burst through the kitchen ceiling. Volunteers managed to rescue the furniture and save a neighbor's house with cellar well water, but Mrs. Harper's house was lost. "On account of a lack of fire fighting apparatus, the building burned to the ground," the *Times*

A horse drawn fire wagon outside the Fire Department Building Number 2 in Mayfield which is now part of Palo Alto.

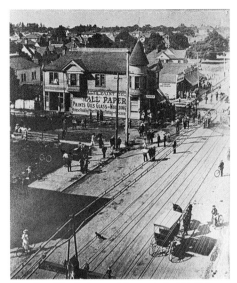

More than 50 onlookers and firemen look at the Palo Alto Paint Company Building—sporting an ad for wallpaper on its side—scene of a fire in 1905.

stated, further speculating that if, "an ax could have been had and a hole had been cut in the roof… the property could have been saved."

After two December fires on University Avenue resulted in more burned buildings, one of the owners, Dr. F. H. Moss, led the formation of a fire association. City business leaders signed up, including John Parkinson and E. C. Thoits, and by April 1896 the city had its first fire-fighting vehicle at the cost of $350. They later added a 131 pound bell for 24 bucks and change.

While Palo Alto now had fire fighters, the volunteer "laddies" did not always perform with the efficiency of the professional fire fighting class. The *Times* commented upon their efforts in April of 1898 with a rather acid tongue: "In Sunday night's fire, the so-called Fire Department succeeded in saving the most valuable part of the property—they saved the lot. Of course the house burned up, but then… a fire in a small town affords a recreation that goes a long way toward dispelling the ennui incidental in living in a village." Harsh.

But there were other times when the boys performed bravely and efficiently, earning positive reviews. When fire broke out at Hemlick's Candy Store at midnight on November 9th, 1904, an entire block of wooden structures was threatened. This time the *Times* was more generous—reporting that "the fire department responded quickly and effectively and within a half an hour the fire was out." Although the candy store was lost, the neighboring Eagle Drug Company was saved, along with a block full of offices, hotels, stables and shops.

But even after the establishment of a department, fires were often a spectator event. They were both a source of excitement and a chance to pitch in—as the paper described when a hay barn fire threatened the house of John Arnott on University Avenue: "Then came the raucous blare of the waterworks whistle… while the bell tolled at City Hall. With that admonition, boys, men, bicycles, autos converged in scattered and hurried rushes toward the scene of excitement."

Chimneys and fireplaces were a frequent source of trouble. In 1899, a spark blew from a nearby chimney to the roof of Miss Emma Kellogg's house. According to accounts, Professor Brun's little boy, who lived next door, yelled to Miss Kellogg to tell her that her roof was on fire. But it was too late. Although fire fighters attached three lines of hose to three hydrants, they could only save the neighboring residence. As the *Palo Alto Live Oak* lamented, "Her home, which has been the scene of so many charming social events, was daintily furnished and contained a fine piano as well as many fine possessions which money cannot replace." The house was completely leveled.

Old-style stoves were also a problem. The culprit of the 1897 fire at the Richmond House at Forest and Bryant was the fire left in the kitchen range. The 15-room, two-story boarding house was locked when neighbors arrived to find the basement in flames and a fire raging inside. Although some $5,000 in property damage was incurred, that figure did not include Mr. V. V. Clark's wardrobe or Mrs. Williams' piano. Clark arrived at the burning house and found that he was refused entrance at the front door. Grabbing a neighbor's ladder, he climbed up to his second-floor residence and saved his trunk and clothing amid the flames. The piano was also rescued in the nick of time after several attempts to liberate it from its first floor location. Mr. A. W. Meany forced his way through the blinding smoke and pushed the piano through the door and out into the hallway where a group of men secured the instrument. Meany then staggered his way out onto the lawn and collapsed in good health but choked exhaustion. It's hard to imagine anyone risking life and limb for a trunk of clothes—or even a piano—these days.

Faulty wiring was another common cause of fires in the early days of Palo Alto. A crossed wire began the 1915 fire at the Ernest Wilson Candy Factory on High Street. $1,500 worth of candy boxes fed the flames that eventually resulted in $25,000 of damage to the candy factory and the W. H. Brooks Bakery next door. The only good news came to neighborhood kids who were able to recover only slightly tinged boxes of chocolates and caramels.

And, of course, overturned lamps were a persistent menace. An April 1898 fire at Lytton and Florence began when a gas lamp was knocked over, producing flames that climbed up cloth-covered walls and quickly spread throughout the unfortunate house. Without a source of water nearby, Mr. A. M. Mayberry daringly braved the flames to rescue his three children, suffering many burns to his hands and face in the process. The Mayberrys had no insurance for their possessions and the family was forced to begin again with nothing to call their own.

Over time, fires would become less of a scourge to Palo Altans and city dwellers across the nation. Safer stoves, lamps and wiring became commonplace while in some areas wooden houses were replaced using less flammable materials. In addition, fire departments perfected their practices and secured better technology to utilize improved water and hydrant systems. So while modern urbanites may be increasingly plagued by crime, pollution and vehicular traffic, they can at least take some comfort that the threat from fires is no longer on the danger shortlist.

A. N. Umphreys and his son, Chester Noble, Harry Vandervoort and others pose on a fire truck just outside the fire station entrance in the city hall bulding on Ramona Street.

A parade through downtown Palo Alto on Independence Day early in the 20th Century.

THE FOURTH OF JULY
Summertime Celebrations

PATRIOTISM IN OUR COUNTRY WAS DIFFERENT A CENTURY AGO. WHILE THERE WERE certainly detractors of the government in the early 1900s, the overall level of trust that Americans had in the nation and its leaders was much higher. It's not necessarily that there is less love of country today, but the nature of the feeling has changed a great deal. It seems we are more critical, more cynical, less wide-eyed in our allegiance these days. Once most Americans seemed to presume that our country was a force for good. Today it seems we're often not so sure.

Widespread confidence lasted well into the 1960s as Ike and JFK led the nation through prosperous years fighting the Red Menace at home and abroad. Polls showed that trust in government was still close to 70% as late as 1966. Enter Vietnam. America's questionable mission in Southeast Asia greatly undermined the public trust, as many began to wonder who the bad guys really were. Publication of the Pentagon Papers and other insider intelligence showed that the government was more than capable of bold-faced lies. Earlier, the civil rights movement had been a wake-up call to many Americans living in the glow of the 1950s—for it was now apparent that not everyone had been living the American Dream. Then came the mother of all government deceptions—Watergate. Since then the Iran-Contra cover-up, the Lewinski affair and the futile search for WMD in Iraq have further added to the skepticism. Today just 25% of Americans say they trust their government. It seems that national patriotism and support for those who are running things are not always in sync.

But a look back at American society a century ago shows a more innocent brand of patriotism—indeed, a more innocent society. For evidence, one can look back at the Independence Day celebrations around the turn of the century. In our city of Palo Alto, for instance, July 4th

A newspaper story about a Palo Alto "Grand Celebration."

The Grand Marshall and aides on horseback during a Mayfield July 4th celebration.

was always a very big deal. And during three summers in particular—1895, 1901 and 1904—the city really pulled out all the stops.

The scale of these events was quite remarkable. For a town incorporated in 1894, the July 4th celebrations were quite ambitious, drawing hundreds of out-of-towners to Palo Alto. They were all-day affairs, beginning at daybreak with the singing of the national anthem and the ceremonial firing of the "National Salute" by two cannons. The 1904 celebration included a parade that stretched over a mile, commencing at 11 o'clock with the explosion of 10,000 powder firecrackers. Holding a thousand small U.S. flags, the marchers proceeded through downtown past houses and storefronts decorated with red, white and blue bunting and patriotic paraphernalia.

The parades always included floats, which were particularly elaborate during the 1895 festivities. On display were national symbols—the Liberty Bell, Uncle Sam, George and Martha Washington and the Goddess of Liberty—accompanied by 44 little girls representing (what were then) "the several states." There was also a "Red Man Float" that would certainly not be appropriate today. The *Palo Alto Times* reported that "the members of the various councils were in Indian costume and their appearance and yells carried one back to the earlier days. Following this were a number of half-naked 'Indian' lads, a squaw with papoose and other appropriate features."

There were great bounties of food. Rather than the family BBQs of today's Fourth of July holiday, the 1904 feast was a community event for no less than 5,000 people. It did feature a similar menu, however. Barbecued meats, along with "assorted delicacies," laid out at tables under a giant red, white and blue tent assembled near the corner of Ramona and University. The 1901 celebration included a free clam bake in which F. S. Gifford, an old-time New Englander, coordinated the baking of 3,000 clams in a brick-lined pit that was heated by a roaring fire.

During the 1904 party the touring Veteran Firemen's Association of San Francisco were featured guests. They demonstrated how fire fighting was done in the "olden days" and performed the song, "When We Ran with the Old Machine." Actually, they weren't kidding—the old machine, in fact, dated back to 1852. In a touching expression of appreciation, 500 of the townspeople marched with the First Regiment Band to Mrs. Jane Stanford's house on campus, serenading her with a tribute to her late husband. She would later call it one of the "landmarks of my life."

Of course, the Fourth of July wouldn't be the same without an exhibition of the national pastime—especially as baseball was never more popular than at the turn of the century. The 1904 match was staged between the Pacific and Western companies of the Southern Pacific Railroad, while in 1901, clerks had a chance to face their bosses away from the store on the diamond.

Those early celebrations were characterized by a lack of self-consciousness hard to imagine today. For instance, patriotic singing was very popular and local citizens didn't hesitate to join the chorus. Along with the "Star-Spangled Banner," Palo Altans also belted out "America," "My Own United States," "American Republic" and "Columbia, the Gem of the Ocean"—an old hymn that for some time was in the running to become our official national anthem. The festivities also featured a trained orator's reading of the Declaration of Independence and a speech from a senator or some other dignitary. In 1895, Dr. Charles Decker rang in the day by exclaiming that "Today from every pulpit, glad, happy people sing their anthems of joy… All the States of the Union have donned their holiday attire and Palo Alto… will permit no locality to out-shine her in her offerings and her enthusiastic display of National love."

There were lots of games—not just for the kids, but for the adults as well. These days it's a little hard to imagine downtown businessmen participating in the "Fat Man's Race," "Doughnut-Eating Contest," or "Three-Legged Pursuit," but it was common in that time. In fact, J. F. Parkinson, future Palo Alto mayor, was the 1901 Fat Man's champ, taking home a coveted box of cigars. Of course it's even harder to imagine the merchants of today queuing up to catch a greased pig, which the 1901 program described as taking place following the animal's "proper lubrication." The event always proved popular since the reward for catching the pig was, in fact, the pig itself.

Non-athletic contests also entertained the crowd. One particular favorite was the "Parade of Horribles," a July 4th tradition common in those days, in which locals dressed up in comically grotesque costumes. Prizes were also awarded for "Best Decorated Bike" and "Best Gentleman Waltzer," although the contests for "Homeliest Woman on the Grounds" and "Best Looking Girl under 14 Years" would probably be left off the program today.

Long after children were in bed, the 1904 holiday carried into the evening with festivities that lasted until one o'clock in the morning. The grand ball, an illuminated bicycle parade, the firing of another 25,000 fireworks and a midnight supper served at two downtown hotels kept stalwart patriots awake and celebrating. Only then was it time to say goodnight to Uncle Sam, thoroughly proving Dr. Decker's earlier prediction that "Palo Alto… will permit no locality to out-shine her in her offerings and her enthusiastic display of National love."

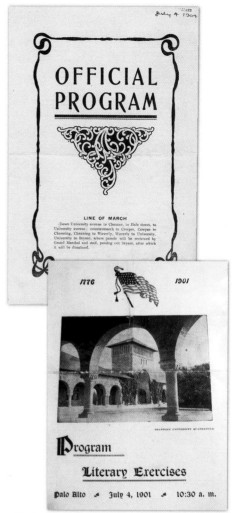

Official programs from July 4th celebrations in Palo Alto in 1904 (top) and 1901 (bottom).

A circus tent going up during Palo Alto's big top heyday. [PALO ALTAN/RON RITTENHOUSE]

THE CIRCUS
The Greatest Show in Palo Alto

There was a time when there was no bigger day in an American small town than Circus Day. It's a little hard to imagine the magnitude of this yearly event now, in part because we've forgotten the remote isolation of small towns in the early part of the 20th century. Before television, radio and the Hollywood movie, small town folk did not have the digitally connected living room that they do today. The geographical isolation was also far more dramatic in those days. Cities had not yet sprawled out into the heartland and the lack of highways and passenger planes meant that millions of Americans would never travel more than a few hundred miles from their place of birth. So when the circus came to town, it was a very big deal. In those days the circus was the only show in town.

Of course Palo Alto was not exactly isolated, even in its earliest incarnation. Not only was it a major university town but it was also just a short train ride away from the biggest city on the West Coast. Still, a look back at pioneer Palo Alto finds a sleepy town that hardly resembles the techie center we know today. Even into the 1930s and '40s—and arguably beyond—Palo Alto was still a quiet little hamlet with the entertainment options to match.

So on circus day, the town came to a virtual halt. *A Palo Alto Times* headline from the 1920s makes this clear by announcing that Palo Alto schools would have a "circus holiday." School authorities, the paper reported, reasoned that "children's minds are not receptive to 'book learning' when the circus is in town."

Of course, the circus was virtually a town of its own. Often taking up two or three dozen railroad cars, the circus arrived at the University Avenue Station. A frantic move would then take place as hundreds of employees would transport the enormous production to one of the circus

A 1935 ad for the Tom Mix Big Three Ring Circus.
[PALO ALTO TIMES]

A 1921 ad for the Palmer Brothers Wild Animal Circus. Dardenella, "The Rose of the Orient" was one of the featured attractions. [PALO ALTO TIMES]

locations—usually an open field. Actually, both of the main Palo Alto circus locations would become future shopping centers—the John Greer property where Town & Country Village now stands and the empty lot where one now finds Edgewood Plaza. Here workers would drive huge spikes into the ground, raise the big top and set up a small city dedicated to laughs and thrills.

A 1936 *Palo Alto Times* story told of the "city within a city" of the 1,080 member Cole Brothers Circus: "This 'city of white tops' which flits around the country has its own postmaster, garage, physician, lawyer, drug store, detectives, barber shop, wheelwright and blacksmith shops."

On the day of the big show, the atmosphere was often hurried and hectic. Usually a circus representative would hustle over to Police Court on Bryant Street to get a permit and invite the fire and safety inspectors back to camp. As Building Inspector Joe Salameda told *Times* editor Elinor Cogswell in her "Editor at Bat" column in 1948, "Everything is hurly-burly. A public relations man takes you over and rushes you around… free passes are being handed out. They capitalize on the confusion." And, of course, heaven help the inspector who actually had to tell the public that the circus had been cancelled.

Many different circuses came through Palo Alto over the years, and they were almost all crowd-pleasers. A look back at some of the touring acts gives a hint of the excitement. Roy Ring's Bicycle Riding Monkey "Tony," Tillie the Fan Dancing Elephant, Dardenella, the Rose of the Orient, Madame Golda and her $10,000 Dancing Horse "White Pearl," and even a pair of "Boxing Horses, direct from England" all delighted the crowds in Palo Alto. Posters advertised the action. Who would want to pass up a chance to see "Clyde Beatty in person shaking dice with death in the big steel cage with 40 cruel, blood-thirsty lions and tigers of opposite sexes"?

But it wasn't always just lions, tigers, clowns and stunts. For instance, when the Barnes Circus arrived in April of 1925, they accompanied traditional acts with a "pageant enacting the adventures of Captain John Smith and his rescue by the Indian Girl Pocahontas." Wild West themes highlighted such shows as the Congress of All-Western Champion Cowboys, Ken Maynard's Wild West, and the 101 Ranch and Wild West Show. The 101 Ranch frantically advertised that the audience would be treated to "An Indian Massacre! A Stage Coach Holdup! And an Outlaw attack on the Emigrant Train!"

Despite the breathless posters and banner headlines, not everything always went exactly as planned. In 1946, for instance, the Clyde Beatty Circus needed the help of police escorts when a railroad strike resulted in the slow plod of the entire circus—pachyderms and all—up El Camino by foot to the next show in Redwood City.

That was nothing compared to the fate of the Palmer Brothers Wild Animal Circus back in November 1921. The entire outfit was stranded in Palo Alto when Mr. Palmer himself took off with all the door receipts as well as the "fat girl, midget maiden, African pigmy boy and Australian bushman," according to the *Palo Alto Times*. Left behind were 190 unpaid employees who took refuge in town waiting for more than $10,000 in past due wages. With Mr. Palmer long gone and no money to keep the circus going, the Times reported days later that many residents were beginning to complain of the "noise of the caged animals" and of "a sanitation problem that has developed." The complaints prompted city authorities to order the circus to leave, charging $100 a day for its use of city land. Eventually, Palmer's abandoned circus was purchased by another proprietor and the animals were deposited at the Palo Alto Stock Farm.

The city always did what it could to help the show. One September night in 1942, local boys were pressed into service when the Cole Brothers Circus arrived short of help because the draft had sent many workers into the army. Each boy received a free pass to the show in exchange for his help. One rainy evening in 1946 several hundred eager Palo Alto children and their parents waited more than an hour for the show to start even though the *Times* reported that "the tent leaked in a thousand places and the ground was ankle deep in mud and straw." Some of those waiting might have recalled that in earlier years, the city served as a winter base for a number of circuses as they retooled before setting out for another tour of the country. Howe's Great London Circus spent four months one winter at the old remount station and spent some $125,000 in town, while during the winter of 1917-1918 the Bernardi Circus's 23 railroad cars parked in Palo Alto.

Eventually, the unique excitement of circus days passed as television, movies, sporting events and other forms of entertainment increasingly dominated. The rising costs of gasoline, big tops, and food for the animals all made travelling circuses an increasingly unprofitable business. In Palo Alto, circus days essentially ended in 1953 with the construction of Town & Country Village. By then the circus Big Top was an endangered species. Eventually the travelling circuses died out, leaving the surviving conglomerates to play indoors in arenas built for ice hockey and basketball. Today's kids see their share of the wonderful and the marvelous on screens big and small, but it's just not the same as sitting a few rows from a dancing elephant or a bicycle-riding monkey.

A 1936 ad for the Barnes Circus.
[PALO ALTO TIMES]

A line of men wait outside the Hotel de Zink during the Depression years. [STANFORD UNIVERSITY ARCHIVES]

THE HOTEL DE ZINK
A Friend Indeed

THE GREAT DEPRESSION WAS LIKE NOTHING AMERICA HAD EVER SEEN. TWENTY-FIVE percent unemployment, eleven thousand bank failures, ten years of hard times. Hundreds of thousands of homeless men roamed the countryside, moving from place to place by hitchhiking or hopping trains, begging for food or work in that era before food stamps or unemployment insurance. They were called hoboes, bums, tramps or stiffs, and by 1931—as the Depression entered its third dark year—it was becoming clear that hungry men were not going away any time soon. City governments began to contemplate what to do with the jobless men who were wandering into town.

For a time, Palo Alto was one of the most progressive cities in the country in providing a helping hand to men riding the rails. But the institution that led the way in the early 1930s was not the brainchild of the mayor or anyone else down at City Hall, but rather the inspiration of Mrs. Mable Glover, who first became interested in the plight of the downtrodden while listening to the Amos 'n' Andy Show.

Tuning into that famous Depression-era radio serial in 1931, Mrs. Glover heard that many restaurants were throwing away leftover food. After a restless night's sleep, Mrs. Glover went down the next day to ask a number of University Avenue restaurant managers if this were true. When she found out that it was, she and her husband, former sea captain Jesse Glover, petitioned the City Council and Mayor C. H. Christensen for money and space to create a shelter. Its mission would be to "assist worthy men who are in distress… using food which is good and wholesome but unsalable."

Jesse and Mable Glover. [PALO ALTO TIMES]

Police Chief Howard Zink was one of the most enthusiastic supporters of the project. [BRUCE CUMMINGS]

The city pitched in $500, use of a truck and an old warehouse on the Federal Telegraph Company property, where the Sheraton Hotel now stands. Soon private donations came pouring in from benevolent Palo Altans, including famed writer Kathleen Norris. Among the shelter's first donations were a hundred cases of canned goods, a full ton of apples, 25 sacks of beets, a live cow and a large bundle of women's underwear.

On November 9th, 1931, the Palo Alto Shelter welcomed its first "knights of the road," almost half of whom had served their country in the armed forces. Before long the shelter would become the Hotel de Zink, to honor Police Chief Howard Zink, an enthusiastic supporter of the project, and to take notice of the building itself, which was partly constructed of steel galvanized with zinc.

The rules of the shelter were strict but fair. Anyone who stayed at the shelter was required to bathe and delouse but also was offered a clean bunk, warm shower, haircut and shave. The hotel's guests were required to work around the shelter and help with upkeep. After a three night stay, the men were asked to move along. Drunkards were not tolerated and Captain Glover oversaw a tight ship. One itinerant described the scene: "When I entered the shelter last night, the first thing I noticed was the behavior of the guests. Usually the transient is noisy and ill-mannered; here he was quiet and reserved. He talked in a low tone of voice, read the newspaper or played cards. When we lined up for supper there was no crowding or shoving. The food was excellent… After the meal, one of the workers asked that the fellows (and he said, 'fellows') pick up the scraps of bread they left at the table. I almost jumped from my seat because he said 'please.' After supper, the crew, the guests and Mrs. Glover sat around the fire and listened to music by three artists of the shelter… it seemed as if a shadow lifted from the hearts of those who were there."

The number of men served by Hotel de Zink was staggering. Records show that in a six-month period from October 1932 to March 1933, the shelter housed some 9,290 men, served 40,881 meals (plus 8,645 second helpings), repaired 948 pairs of shoes, gave out 1,680 pairs of socks and even provided 111 three-piece suits. The shelter also served the local poor, delivering Christmas baskets, preparing 1,360 lunches for local children and giving out wood and clothes to needy Palo Altans. Shelter services included a small 13-bed hospital overseen by Dr. John Silliman, meals prepared by the former chef of Monterey's Hotel Del Monte grill (like the Glovers, he took no salary), as well as a shoe repair shop (many men came into the shelter in bare feet), tailor shop, small barber shop, newspaper and dentist.

Sadly, as the Depression wore on, some Palo Altans lost patience with funding the Hotel de Zink. Complaints were heard that the shelter was diverting too much charity to out-of-towners and not enough to locals in need. The shelter was criticized for hiring non-Palo Altans to their staff during a time when jobs were beyond scarce. There were protests demanding that itinerants be sent on to San Francisco or San Jose.

In April of 1934, after two and a half years of assisting out-of-work men, the shelter closed. For another five years, it labored on in a limited capacity, serving meals in exchange for work. The Glovers continued to give elsewhere to those in need. Mrs. Glover supervised a large San Francisco shelter, while "Cap" Glover helped institute shelters up and down the state.

Today the name Hotel de Zink has been revived by InnVision/Urban Ministry for an emergency shelter that rotates among local churches. Though its scale is nothing like the original, the name is a tribute to Depression visitors and the Palo Altans who met each other at the old shelter. For some of the 50,000 weary men it served, the first Hotel de Zink was remembered as a comfort to them in their hardest days. One man later wrote to Captain and Mrs. Glover: "To the best friends I have. May your years be long and happy and you enjoy life and may God bless you. As a friend in need, you were a friend indeed."

Below left: Hotel de Zink construction [SAN FRANCISCO NEWS, NOVEMBER 2, 1931]

Below right: A barber gives a guest a haircut inside the shelter. [FREDERIC O. GLOVER]

The March 13, 1939 front page [PALO ALTO TIMES]

MARCH 13, 1939
A Day in the Life

HISTORY IS OFTEN PRESENTED COMPARTMENTALLY IN ORDER TO EXPLAIN COMPLICATED events. Take a look at any daily newspaper and you get an understanding of the cacophony of stories that occupy a single historical moment—and how they interrelate.

In this spirit, it may be interesting to capture a snapshot of another era by looking back at life in Palo Alto through one day's newspaper. Rolling back the microfilm of the *Palo Alto Times*, let's turn back the clock more than 70 years to a day when Depression hardships were still familiar to Palo Altans. Welcome to the clear and bright morning of March 13, 1939.

Looking at the front page, we notice that America was very focused on world events. While more than two and a half years would pass before Pearl Harbor pulled us into World War II, there was no doubt that Palo Altans were concerned with international affairs. The front page speaks to a world increasingly out of control. The top headline concerns a Slovak riot in the Czechoslovakian city of Bratislava, sponsored by Nazi Germany across the border. The next day the Slovak Parliament split from the Czechoslovakian government to form the Slovak Republic, giving ally Nazi Germany a base for later attacks on Poland..

Fear and anticipation of war are noticeable in other sections of the paper. That day's Op-Ed section, for instance, includes a letter from an Olga K. Robinson of Palo Alto, who voices her disapproval of the administration in Washington: "Any hope for a long continued peace, if you call our present condition peace, seems hopeless with President Roosevelt straining every nerve to protect our frontiers from Guam to Germany." The sense of Fascism on the march is present in a *Times* editorial on local Girl Scouts: "In a world threatened by totalitarian philosophies, regimentation and mass thinking, the Girl Scout movement stands for the development of individuality."

The offices of the Palo Alto Times were for many years located at the corner of Hamilton and Ramona.

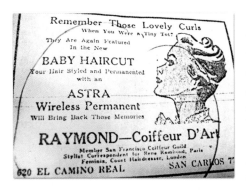

Haircuts and chips were some of the items advertised in the March 13, 1939, edition. [PALO ALTO TIMES]

In an interesting front page juxtaposition, affairs abroad are just a column away from scientific discoveries concerning the very nature of the universe. A small front-page article carries this rather bold headline: "Einstein: He Discovers Law of Gravity." The story then goes on to detail the professor's interview with L. E. Levick of the National Association of Science Writers and explains that "Einstein thinks he has discovered the clue to a long sought single law that will explain the structure of the entire universe and all the mysteries of matter and radiation." Pretty big news for a sidebar column.

In local news of the day, accidents were a common theme. You'll find a shocking number of stories in old newspapers telling of freak misfortune—car crashes, death by drowning, electrocution and a great many child deaths. In the days before guard rails, seat belts, child-proofing and increased government safety intervention, such events were an unfortunate reality of life. The March 13 Palo Alto paper is no different, telling of a car crash at Lytton and Middlefield while an Op-Ed letter calls for an underpass at California Avenue to avoid "needless tragedies… such as the one that occurred Monday at the California railroad crossing."

You can also see how much our community has changed by looking beyond the front page. A scan of the classifieds on page 8 turns up some interesting items. The great differences in prices—especially Depression prices—are always a bit startling. For instance, a trip to the Lincoln Garage on El Camino Real—"1 mile south of Mayfield on the highway"—could net you an eight-year-old Buick sedan for a hundred bucks or a one-year-old pick-up for just $17.50. A four-bedroom house in the Walter Hays neighborhood was going for $9,500, and if you wanted to give it a fresh coat of paint, you could pick some up for just $1.35 a gallon.

Other items in the classified section date Palo Alto as still somewhat rustic in 1939. For instance, it would be hard to imagine finding classified ads in today's paper for "the removal of dead or live stock," "Winchester Hi Quality Chicks: hatching every Thursday" or even "an analysis of whether your soil is sweet or sour."

Newspaper standbys were also different. In this pre-television era, the *Times* carried daily radio listings below a diagram of "Your Dial," showing the call number of each station. Remarkably, one of the shows still looks familiar. Radio soap opera "Guiding Light" ran locally on KPO in 1939. Eventually moving to the tube, it became the longest-running TV drama in history.

Serial stories in written form were also popular newspaper features. The paper would publish a new chapter daily and the reader would check in for the very latest. "Mrs. Doc" by Tom Horner is featured in the March 13th paper—as the action is picked up in Chapter 5. The "Funnies, Fads and Features" section includes a Movie Scrapbook, with personality tidbits on stars such as Nigel Bruce and Dorothy Lovett, as well as a "Kwiz Korner" and an extensive page of cartoons. While most of the comic strips are similar to those found today, one cartoon, "Myra North, Special Nurse," displays the ugly stereotypes of the era. The strip's namesake is a black mammy housekeeper who is characterized in the unfortunate style often given to black servants in that time. In one line Myra remarks to her employer: "Lawdy-lawdy! Jes' look at 'dis shirt Mistah Freddy…"

The society page certainly has a different feel as well. Mary Hampton's fashion column discusses whether "it is right for a high school girl to wear her shirt-tails hanging out." Concluding that it is not, she praises local schools that regulate such behavior, writing "When a school steps in to guide girls, I think they are doing something very valuable for the girls' future."

And there are other little tidbits throughout the paper that show how much things have changed. Ads for "the Shaw Motor Co." and "Carlson's Home Made Candy" display four-digit phone numbers—"Dial 3179," one ad encourages. There are also little differences in language and fashion. An ad for Blue Bird Potato Chips shows a store clerk in a bow tie proclaiming "Folks—they're tops!" above a blue bird wearing a fedora. And Raymond Coiffeur D'Art on University Avenue asks women to "remember those lovely curls" of youth as it promotes "The Baby Haircut"—the Astra Wireless Permanent. Married women were often identified by their husbands' names, in a way that seems rather insulting today. For instance, the March 13th paper reports that a turnabout party was held at the Palo Alto Yacht Club for Mrs. Fred Hage. And it's also interesting, if a bit troubling, that regular citizens are often identified by their home addresses. You certainly don't see that anymore.

Not everything is different. Closing our microfilm version of the paper's final page, we see listings of scores for Stanford, Paly and Elks games much as we might today. There are ads for businesses still in operation such as the Peninsula Creamery and the Palo Alto Sport Shop. And movie listings for the Stanford Theatre and invitations to shop on University Avenue remind us that while customs and styles vary with time, the essential spirit of the city is what it always was.

Shaw Motor Company, car dealer and gas station at Forest and High Streets (above) also placed an ad in the March 13, 1939, issue. [PALO ALTO TIMES]

The unfortunate comic strip, "Myra North, Special Nurse" was also in the March 13, 1939, edition.

Palo Alto's Civil Defense, World War II.

PALO ALTO'S CIVIL DEFENSE
Panic After Pearl Harbor

IN THE CONFUSING DAYS AFTER THE DECEMBER 7TH, 1941 ATTACK ON PEARL HARBOR, CITIES all over the Pacific Coast were in a state of panic. The destruction of nine warships and 188 aircraft in Hawaii left 2,350 Americans dead and the country greatly unsettled. It was feared that the West Coast stood completely defenseless and terrified civilians braced themselves for the possibility of Japanese troops storming California beaches. Even when a second wave did not come, Californians continued to maintain vigilant and organized civilian defense throughout the war.

Looked at decades later with a certain amount of victorious historical hindsight, an American continent bordered on both sides by vast oceans seems rather impenetrable. But after the profound shock of Pearl Harbor, the possibility of a Japanese attack on the U.S. mainland seemed all too plausible—especially in the Bay Area. As rumors were flying everywhere, hours after the initial Japanese strike, a report came into the Army's Western Defense Command that a Japanese fleet was just thirty miles off the San Francisco coast. Sixty Army trucks raced to the water below the Golden Gate Bridge to install anti-aircraft guns and by nightfall, every available soldier at the Presidio was digging trenches on the beach. Meanwhile, on the Bay Bridge, a jittery sentry seriously wounded a female driver who was slow to stop at an improvised checkpoint. Similar episodes played out across the nation. In Los Angeles, antiaircraft battery shot at imaginary planes, injuring dozens of Southlanders as the shells fell upon the city. And as air raid sirens directed citizens on the West Coast to turn out their lights in preparation for a Japanese air attack that never came, a mob of 1,000 angry Seattleites smashed windows and looted stores that remained illuminated. Indeed, while Franklin Roosevelt was resolutely declaring December 7, "a date which will live in infamy," much of the nation was more than a little frazzled.

Mayor Blois set up a committee on disaster preparedness and relief in Palo Alto.

The Civil Defense Administration invited Americans on the home front to help with the fight. [WIKIPEDIA COMMONS/NATIONAL ARCHIVES AND RECORDS ADMINISTRATION, 1941–1945]

Palo Alto also was on edge. In the hours after Pearl Harbor, an antiaircraft battery stood atop a hill near Page Mill Road and what is now Foothill Expressway, searching the skies for enemy attack planes. And like most of the West Coast, Palo Alto stood in darkness that night (and many to follow) as military strategists feared that city lights would provide easy targets for Japanese bombers. Meanwhile, Palo Alto police rushed to secure utilities plants, the water reservoir and the airport, while the City Council met by emergency flashlight. Perhaps some of this local panic was what prompted an editorial in the *Palo Alto Times* on December 8 headlined, "This is not a time for any form of hysteria; calm and disciplined action is needed now."

Over the next few days, Mayor Byron Blois set up a committee on disaster preparedness and relief. The committee called for volunteers to serve as emergency police, asking others for voluntary time through a service questionnaire. Meanwhile, Palo Alto Police Chief Howard Zink organized an auxiliary group to support the police, even soliciting donations of ".38 special Smith and Wesson or Colt revolvers… so that men donating their services can be properly equipped." The Palo Alto Red Cross was also moved to action, asking for the help of "any persons owning station wagons which could be used for emergency ambulances." Meanwhile a group of 45 "radio hams" organized the Palo Alto Amateur Radio Club to help local relief workers communicate using ultra-high frequency equipment.

Blackouts soon became a regular part of life in Palo Alto. Although University Avenue merchants reported a run on all sorts of blackout materials from dark green window shades to black oilcloth, it took some time for city residents to get accustomed to the practice. "Incomplete cooperation" in three Palo Alto blackouts on December 9 led City Engineer L. Harold Anderson to write up a list of thirteen rules for air raids to run on the front page of the *Palo Alto Times* the following day. A few nights later, less than 100% compliance resulted in the plug being pulled on light switches controlling the entire city after just fifteen minutes. Part of the wayward behavior was probably due to the variation in signals being used in different Bay Area cities. Residents close to the Menlo Park line, for instance, reported a confusing din of various blasts with different meanings on different sides of the border. The City Council had little sympathy, however, imposing a penalty of up to six months in jail and a $500 fine for those who did not comply.

Blackouts eventually became more polished as the Civil Defense Administration in Washington helped unify localities. In Palo Alto, wardens were selected for each block to make sure that all house and car lights in the area were extinguished. The *Palo Alto Times* of December 30, 1941, published the official text of "A Handbook for Air Wardens," which stated their war time mission: "You are the embodiment of all civilian defense… It will be your responsibility to see that everything possible is done to protect and safeguard those homes and citizens from the new hazards created by attack from the air or enemies from within our gates."

Palo Altans were also trained in what to do if they found themselves in the midst of an attack. On May 11, 1942, for instance, the *Palo Alto Times* printed a special "Civilian Defense Handbook" edition—"Study it and keep it near for reference," a subheadline advised. The special edition was complete with articles from local officials including William Clemo, chief of the Palo Alto Fire Department, and Howard Zink, head of the Police Department. One article about poisonous gas cited the expertise of Dr. Charles E. Shepard warning that "it is quite possible that the enemy may use some form of gas to terrorize citizens if bombing occurs on the West Coast." The article went on to counsel on coping with mustard gas, describing how to treat oneself with naphtha laundry soap, among other household items.

Another article advised Palo Altans what to do if "a fire bomb pays you a call" and how to set up a "blackout room." But the paper's recommendation for how to effectively treat the injured or the ill was perhaps a bit curt—"Try to take care of the emergency yourself. After all, this is war." And some rather metaphysical guidance appeared on page eight, in which an AP science editor advocated that those on the home front should practice walking blindfolded toward a wall. "You can learn in that way how to sense the wall before bumping against it," the article reasoned.

As the threat of an actual Japanese attack on American soil began to recede, panic subsided and the nation stirred into action. As the country transformed itself into a wartime economic machine, this industrial juggernaut that FDR called "the arsenal of democracy" would eventually make the difference in providing victory to the Allies.

Still, there is no doubt that in the wake of Pearl Harbor, America reeled in shock as it was drawn out of isolation by a determined foe. Forced to organize itself for war, the nation pulled together and began an epic mobilization and comeback that transformed the attack on Pearl Harbor from a daringly brilliant military tactic to a decisively dreadful mistake.

Posters and propaganda reminded Americans of the loss at Pearl Harbor. [WIKIPEDIA COMMONS/ NATIONAL ARCHIVES AND RECORDS ADMINISTRATION, 1941–1945]

War stamps and bonds were sold in Palo Alto, as shown here at the University Avenue Train Station.

THE PALO ALTO HOME FRONT
Life During Wartime

WHEN THE JAPANESE ATTACKED PEARL HARBOR ON DECEMBER 7, 1941, THEY AWOKE a sleeping giant—the American economic machine that Franklin Roosevelt had once called, "the arsenal of democracy." Although the United States had been mired in ten years of economic depression and was initially weary of war, it rallied to counter the humiliation of Pearl Harbor. The country soon began a steady progression toward the massive wartime economy that would eventually affect almost every aspect of life on the home front. In many ways, this domestic transformation was just as important as the fighting taking place overseas. For once America's mighty economic engine had been ignited; defeat was more or less in the cards for its enemies.

What war meant to Americans at home was different during World War II than in any subsequent American war. From Korea to Vietnam to the Gulf War, Afghanistan and Iraq, Americans have had the luxury of sending off their military personnel without much change in their own daily lives. But the sheer size and scope of the Second World War meant that every American got the call from Uncle Sam in one way or another.

As a West Coast city, Palo Alto was heavily involved in the war effort. The city certainly sent its share of soldiers overseas: from Palo Alto High School alone, 73 graduates died for their country. But those back home were also invited—sometimes virtually compelled—by the government to do their part. A review of wartime posters finds that Palo Altans, like the rest of country, were called upon to "buy war bonds," "take your place in civil defense," "share the meat," "save your tires," "eat the right food," even "button your lip."

A war bond drive at the Stanford Theatre during World War II.

Still, America's propaganda machine spoke what was an essential truth—the key to American victory lay in the effort of civilians at home. And indeed that word "victory" seemed to be everywhere. Americans were asked to drive at special "victory speeds" to save rubber—just 35 mph on the highways. The government urged Americans to prepare "victory homes," which according to ads from the Palo Alto Hardware Company necessitated essentials such as the Plumb Defensax, an air raid safety tool in case of foreign attack. Men wore "victory suits" that used less cotton by fashioning narrow lapels and short coats while an Office of Price Administration "victory cookbook" offered meals heavy on non-rationed ingredients.

The youth of Palo Alto helped out in "rubber drives" throughout World War II.

Of course, there were also the famed "victory gardens" in which average Americans helped protect the public food supply by growing their own vegetables in the backyard. Originally promoted by Secretary of Agriculture Claude R. Wickard as a civil morale booster, more than twenty million victory gardens flourished nationwide including hundreds in Palo Alto. In October 1943, Jordan Junior High Schoolers boasted a victory garden that produced "one ton of foodstuff—the amount an average soldier consumes in a year."

And there were still other ways that those on the home front could contribute. Housewives saved kitchen fat in jars, which later could be turned into the glycerin used in explosives. In one

A Palo Alto "Victory Garden."

Liberty magazine spread, two sailors ogled elegant Hollywood actress Helen Hayes handing a jar of fat to a grocer as she told housewives that "a single pound of kitchen grease will make two anti-aircraft shells." And kids found they were essential as well in scrounging for metals and rubber for scrap drives. Local kids peeled foil out of cigarette packs and gum wrappers while wearing government issued banners reading "Slap the Jap right off the map by Salvaging Scrap!"

Palo Altans, like all Americans, were called to sacrifice during the war years. Volunteer workers at the Palo Alto Ration Board placed limits on such items as sugar, meat, butter, coffee, gasoline, tires—even typewriters. The strict limitations on driving led to a comeback by the bicycle. The *Palo Alto Times* reported to readers that "the automobile replaced the horse and now the bicycle has replaced the automobile." Crammed racks of bikes were everywhere along University

"The World's Only Puppet Rodeo Show" helped sell War Bonds in Palo Alto.

Avenue during the war years as tire rationing was severe. During the month of February 1942 the entire city was allowed just eighteen car tires. And Palo Altans had to get used to going without. The *Times* reported that "folks wait weeks for laundry without a peep for fear of being cut off the driver's list" while "shoes wait weeks for repair in local cobbler shops short of help."

With so much of the nation's workforce on battlefields in Europe and at sea in the South Pacific, the American labor market saw wholesale changes. Famously, women were pressed into traditionally male roles from bank tellers to factory workers. Still, it was hard to forget that such advances were due more to necessity than open minds. A 1944 *Palo Alto Times* news piece sounds a rather patronizing tone: "Many a man realizes now how competent the girls are at his old jobs. In [Palo Alto] they have pitched in and 'manned' taxis, buses, the cannery, gas stations, the banks, the post office. Let 'em stay on after the war, we say, leaving the men to hunt and fish—as God intended." And a 1943 article exclaimed that "it's fashionable to be useful, as well as beautiful, this year." The story told of nearly forty Palo Alto women training for jobs at Bay Area war plants.

Other women served as volunteers. Hundreds of housewives rolled bandages for the Palo Alto Red Cross, while one Palo Altan, Mrs. Walter Rodgers (as she was always identified in the press) opened "Hospitality House" in her own residence, tallying a guest book registration of over 50,000 by 1944. During the 1943 Christmas she organized the transport to soldiers abroad of some 700 individually-wrapped gifts donated by Palo Altans.

Finally, a little after four on the afternoon of August 14, 1945, reports began to circulate throughout the city that the Japanese had surrendered. As in most parts of the country, an impromptu party immediately broke out. A city siren appropriately malfunctioned and blared for a quarter of an hour as firecrackers were lit and makeshift confetti thrown. One woman gleefully marched down University Avenue banging a milk bottle against an ice cream freezer and cars packed with young men from Stanford's army training corps—some in full battle regalia—rolled into town with horns honking. Youngsters ripped American flags from J.C. Penney's and the Hotel President and waved them excitedly while the Stanford Band marched down University Avenue to the Stanford Theatre where they triumphantly played "The Star Spangled Banner." At last it was all over. After more than three and a half years of rations, shortages, blackouts and worries, success was finally at hand. Victory had been hard-earned, peace had arrived, the future was bright.

"Boom Town" and "The Great Lover" are among the features in this Palo Alto Drive-In flier, from February 1950.

THE PALO ALTO DRIVE-IN
A Generational Memory

KIDS RUNNING THE BASES THESE DAYS AT GREER PARK HAVE NO KNOWLEDGE THAT THEIR ballfield was once a theatre—the old Palo Alto Drive-In Movie Theatre. For those of a certain age, the drive-in theatre stirs up memories of halcyon days of teenage revelry, backseat love affairs, and Hollywood's epic years. While for the generations that followed, the whole concept of watching a movie in your car is a little hard to imagine.

The first person to imagine it was the sales manager at Camden, New Jersey's Whiz Auto Products, Richard M. Hollingshead, Jr. After hearing his rather large mother complain one too many times about the slightness of movie theatre seats, Hollingshead experimented with projecting movies in his backyard. With a bedsheet nailed to two trees, he used a 1928 Kodak projector and a radio to entertain a few guests. Playing with the concept, Hollingshead propped up neighborhood cars on cinderblocks until he had a design for the perfect car ramp. It's hard to imagine a simpler idea, but on May 16th, 1933, he received Patent #1,909,537 for his design of a ramp to allow passengers parked in cars to see over the roofs of those in front. In 1941, improved technology replaced large speakers with small movable ones attached to posts next to each car—the drive-in movie was ready for the big time. By 1958, there were more than 4,000 drive-ins nationwide.

The Peninsula Drive-In Theatre opened off old Bayshore Highway in 1947. An ad in the *Palo Alto Times* beckoned viewers to "see the stars—under the stars" while promoting the opening's double feature—Shirley Temple's "Kiss and Tell" and a Disney cartoon, "Make Mine Music."

The Peninsula Drive-In (later renamed the Palo Alto Drive-In) consisted of a 70-foot screen —said to be the largest in the western states at the time—a snack bar, central projection house, and semi-circular ramp with the capacity to hold 750 cars. And the requisite small speakers could

Originally the drive-in was known as the Peninsula Drive-In, as in this flier from 1947.

When drive-in movies were king

A 1986 aerial photo of the old Palo Alto Drive-in shows its location next to the Bayshore Freeway. [PALO ALTAN/ LUTHER GIPSON]

be hung inside the car (an announcement after the show urgently reminded viewers to put the speakers back in the receptacle before driving off). Indeed, at just 60¢ per adult, 14¢ per child and "no charge for your car," the Drive-In was one of Palo Alto's most economical nights out.

Drive-ins primarily appealed to two different segments of American society. They were perfect for parents who could bring their little ones along in the backseat (sometimes already in PJs) and enjoy a movie without paying for a sitter. For teens, the drive-in offered a bit of much-desired privacy—especially if you parked way in the back. A Nat King Cole song of the era proclaimed that at the drive-in "you'll see more kisses in the car than on the screen," and often kissing was just the beginning of the festivities. By the mid-'50s the adults had caught on, and drive-ins were condemned as "passion pits" by disapproving clergy. In Palo Alto, as in other drive-ins, employees were known to patrol the lot, shining flashlights into cars when no heads were visible.

Indeed, in some ways drive-in theatres were never really about the movies. After all, your front windshield probably wasn't the best showcase for the world's cinematic masterpieces. The movies tended to be big and brash—Hollywood at its most gargantuan. Palo Alto Drive-In fliers of the day advertise such long forgotten B-movies as "Wildfire" ("with thundering hoofs and thundering guns!"), "Summer Holiday," ("a big Technicolor Musical!") and "Stampede" ("Roaring out of the Lusty West!"). One flier boasts pictures of Tyrone Power proclaiming, "I will use a woman's lips as I use a sword… to conquer." Yes, not exactly "Citizen Kane."

Ironically, even as the movies got bigger and bigger, it was a smaller screen that would help bring down the drive-in. After reaching peak numbers in the late 1950s, close to 700 drive-ins would close over the next fifteen years, including Palo Alto's. And as daylight savings time, color television, the VCR and Cable TV all came into their own, drive-ins began to close up shop in the 1970s. By 1987, there were fewer than 1,000 in operation nationwide and only about 400 today.

While many drive-in owners sold their land for housing or offices, Palo Alto's drive-in became a park. After closing, neighborhood activists lobbied the City to purchase the land and combine it with Amarillo Park to form a larger park. Over the next twenty years Palo Alto constructed the Greer Park in phases—adding softball fields, basketball courts and eventually a skate park at its southern edge. Today a visit to Greer Park provides no hint that these grounds once hosted a storied slice of Americana. In Palo Alto—as in much of America—the drive-in movie lives on primarily in the minds of those who were there.

CHANGING TIMES

A postcard image of the Varsity Theatre on University Avenue, circa 1920s. [THE CAROLYN PIERCE POSTCARD COLLECTION]

PATERNALISM AT THE MOVIES
Palo Alto's Commercial Board of Amusements

IN THE EARLY DAYS OF CINEMA, BEFORE HOLLYWOOD ESTABLISHED ITS OWN PRODUCTION code to govern violence and sexuality on the screen, the moving picture business was essentially unregulated. Fearing the worst, some localities, including Palo Alto, created their own boards of regulation. Beginning in 1921, the Advisory Board of Commercial Amusements would spend the next three decades holding sway over what Palo Altans could see on the big screen.

Those who remember classic movies as tame soft-focus love serenades may not be aware of Hollywood's earlier "decade of debauchery." In the 1920s, actresses often appeared on screen in their underwear or even nude, and early talkies used "damn" and "son of a bitch." On-screen topics included prostitution, homosexuality, illegal drug use and miscegenation. While these no-nos probably wouldn't make many contemporary moviegoers blush, they were utter blasphemy compared to the conventions of the following era.

A series of scandals inched Hollywood toward the production code. In 1921, Fatty Arbuckle stood trial accused of manslaughter in the death of actress Virginia Rappe at an out-of-control San Francisco party. His acquittal did not erase sensational publicity. The murder next year of director William Desmond Taylor and the revelations about his bisexuality and the drug-related death of actor Wallace Reid in 1923 further demoted Hollywood's reputation around the nation. Throughout the Roaring Twenties, the combination of daring on and off-screen behavior had the public demanding action.

Fearing regulation of the movies from the federal government, Hollywood decided to regulate itself. In 1930, the major studios adopted a Production Code to spell out what was acceptable on the screen. Written by a Jesuit priest (appropriately named Father Daniel A. Lord), Code

The Advisory Board of Commercial Amusement's recommendations were always kept on file for perusal at Palo Alto's Carnegie Library on Hamilton Avenue.

Section of a full-page listing of ads for the Palo Alto Drive-In theatre, 1950. At the bottom of the page a disclaimer states, "program subject to change."

enforcement began in earnest in July of 1934. It would prove nearly impenetrable for more than 30 years, governing Hollywood films with specific rules banning profanity and nudity as well as edicts prohibiting the portrayal of religious ministers as comic characters or villains. The Code sought to put an end to "morally ambiguous endings" and it was also decreed that the "sympathy of the audience should never be thrown to the side of crime, wrongdoing, evil or sin."

Still, by the time Hollywood got around to censoring itself, cities like Palo Alto already had their own system in place. By its second year, the Advisory Board of Commercial Amusements had already banned all of Fatty Arbuckle's comedies to date, despite his acquittal. By way of explanation, the Board turned the tradition of "innocent until proven guilty" on its head, maintaining that they would not approve "the showing in Palo Alto of any films featuring any actor or actress who had gained unsavory notoriety by reason of alleged viciousness in private life."

After the 1920s, the Board put in place a procedure for passing judgment that lasted until 1954. On a weekly basis, Board members perused reviews of new films in bulletins such as the confidently-titled, *Unbiased Opinions of Current Motion Pictures*. If the reviews persuaded three or more members of the seven-member volunteer Board that the film might "tend to corrupt the public morals" then a preview would be ordered—to be screened at the theatre's expense, no less. If the Board restricted a film in Palo Alto, copies of the judgment went straight to the Palo Alto Police. The threat to revoke a theatre's license for showing the banned movie ensured that in practice theatre owners were always compliant throughout the Board's 33-year run.

In fairness, the Board was mainly an advisory panel, putting movies into categories such as "family," "young people" or "adults only." In a number of op-eds and statements over the years, the Board contended that it would not get involved in "Thou Shall Not" censorship, but rather would engage in aiding parents in making informed decisions. Such weekly recommendations were published for many years in the *Palo Alto Times* and were available at the reference desk at the downtown Carnegie Library.

The Board also kept an eye on horror films. In 1952, the Board asked theatre owners not to double-bill children's films with adult horror films, as was sometimes the practice on Saturdays. The Board banned outright 38 horror films in Palo Alto between 1943 and 1954. Given that the current rating system of PG-13 and R rated films would not be established for more than 15 years, it made sense that a civic group would provide this service to Palo Alto parents.

Yet there were many cases where the Board's editing or banning of movies crossed the line into censorship. This was particularly the case in the 1950s. Although by that time Palo Alto was one of just two California cities to have an advisory system in place (the other was in Pasadena), the Board seemed intent on reviewing scenes which challenged the Code. In the late '40s, "The Outlaw" and "Duel in the Sun" were banned until certain scenes were snipped. In 1954, "The City Across the River," "I the Jury," "Man Crazy," and "La Ronde" were all banned outright. A film called "Donovan's Brain" was also censored because of the Board's questionable critique that "it depicts people as worse than they really are." The Board also struck down "The French Line," a Jane Russell film with a plot that seems to have centered a great deal around her cleavage. Sexy vehicles for Rita Hayworth, Jane Russell and Jayne Mansfield had become well known for pushing the boundaries of the Code.

Although the Hollywood Production Code did not break until the late 1960s, it began to bend in the 1950s. Spurred on by a 1952 Supreme Court decision that movies were protected by the First Amendment—a 1915 decision had found that they were not—theatres began to challenge the Advisory Board's authority. On March 4, 1954, California Avenue's Cardinal Theatre owner Alfred Laurice sued the City in Superior Court, claiming that the Board's pronouncements violated the Constitution. Among the complaints from Laurice and other theatre owners —such as George Archibald of the Palo Alto Drive-in Theatre—was the claim that obligatory previews could cost the theatre owner as much as $50, making it difficult to compete with Menlo Park movie houses that could show the films free of hassle. On March 22, City Councilman Lee Rodgers received the backing of the *Palo Alto Times* editorial page when he offered a motion to abolish the Board entirely.

Indeed, it seemed that the Board's time had passed. Although it held on for some time in strictly an advisory capacity, the Board eventually stopped meeting altogether. City paternalism, it seemed, had grown out of fashion. Ten years later the Hollywood Production Code would also fall, challenged at first by films from overseas and then by American films made outside the studio system. By the late '60s, all bets were off at the movie theatres as a new era of sexual mores was in full bloom. A new era more concerned with personal choice and freedom had begun and anything that smacked of censorship was on its way out.

The Aquarius Theatre in 1969 after the Commercial Board was no longer reviewing film content.

Woolworth's at its original location on University Avenue next to the Elite Market, circa 1920s.

WOOLWORTH'S
Palo Alto's Five and Dime

IN RECENT YEARS, WALMART HAS TAKEN A BEVY OF VERBAL ATTACKS FROM SMALL TOWN merchants and competition watchdogs. The complaint stands that America's biggest retail outlet moves into small towns, undercuts local prices and puts Main Street "Mom & Pops" out of business. But while the economic gigantism of Walmart may damage any sense of free market justice in small town America, such complaints were heard about other stores long before Sam Walton ever started lowering smiley-faced sticker prices. For decades it was the F. W. Woolworth's store on every American Main Street that had local shop owners muttering about out-of-town corporate bullies. Here in Palo Alto, department stores like Bergmann's, I. Magnin's and The Emporium eventually had long runs outside downtown, but for 70 years, it was F. W. Woolworth's that was the place to get just about everything.

Frank Winfield Woolworth began his business career with a couple of big ideas. When he opened the original Woolworth's, it was one of the first department stores to put the merchandise out on the floor. Up until then, customers would hand their shopping lists to a clerk who fetched the items from behind the counter—usually leading to some negotiation over price. Woolworth also tried to rewrite the economic playbook customary to department stores. Slashing prices to almost ridiculous lows, F. W. attempted to simply sell as many goods as possible, trusting that profits would follow.

And indeed they did. After an initial failed start on a $300 loan, F. W. Woolworth's "five and dime" model prospered in the 1880s, originally in Lancaster, Pennsylvania, and later across the nation. Soon F. W. was on his way to realizing his stated goal of putting red and gold awnings "in every town of over 10,000 in the country."

Frank Winfield Woolworth, one of the most successful businessmen of the 20th Century. [WIKIPEDIA COMMONS]

The majestic Woolworth's Building in New York City. [WIKIPEDIA COMMONS/U.S. LIBRARY OF CONGRESS, CIRCA 1913]

The riches that came to Woolworth made him one of the richest men in America—and one of the most extravagant. Mourning the death of his daughter and the illness of his wife, Woolworth embarked on a seemingly desperate attempt to cure his depression through material satisfaction. He built an entire row of mansions for his daughters on New York's Fifth Avenue, as well as a mansion on Long Island that included a room-sized pipe organ, a $2 million pink marble staircase, and a full-time staff of 70 gardeners. The gaudy spending spree culminated with the $13 million Woolworth Building, which was paid for entirely in cash and was erected in 1911 as the world's tallest building.

After Woolworth's death in 1919, the company continued to prosper under the savvy guidance of the company board—his boys, as F. W. had referred to them. While inflation eventually forced the stores to raise prices above a dime, Woolworth's continued to expand and thrive in the Great Depression and through the mid-20th century. The introduction of the famed Woolworth's lunch counters further attracted customers. The red stools and grilled hot dogs, chicken soup and milkshakes— all helped pioneer the teaming of food and shopping which became second nature to stores like Ikea, Target and Borders Books. And in the days before malls and drive-ins, the Woolworth's counter was a popular hangout spot in virtually every American small town.

In 1917, Palo Alto got its own Woolworth's. The original location was at 222 University Avenue, and its opening was a big event for a small town. A musical orchestra greeted customers at a special dedication in which hundreds of customers turned out just to "look over" the merchandise before the store officially opened for business the following day. In those early days, Woolworth's sold many items recognizable today—though at much cheaper prices. A look back at old newspaper ads reveals that you could get three pencils for a nickel, a baseball for a dime and a mirror for just fifteen cents. Today's shoppers would be less familiar with other items for sale, such as dust caps, jelly tumblers and tatting shuttles.

In 1949, Woolworth's moved to 352 University Avenue, the 185-foot-long building now occupied by CVS Pharmacy. The opening was again a big deal, bringing out the mayor, fire chief, chief of police, and president of the Chamber of Commerce. They helped usher in the brand new building that featured such novelties as air conditioning, fluorescent lighting and a new lunch counter and soda fountain. And with the longest frontage along University Avenue, this new Woolworth's store would anchor the University Avenue shopping district for the next four decades.

And yet customers across the country in the 1950s were heading out of downtown for the convenience of suburban malls. Woolworth's went with them. In Palo Alto, this progression took shoppers away from University Avenue and out to the newly finished Stanford Shopping Center. While the downtown location remained, a new Woolworth's opened in 1955 as one of 11 original tenants in the shopping center.

Of course, in those days the Stanford Shopping Center was more like a neighborhood mall than the regional luxury center of chic that it would later become. The shopping center's early incarnation—which included a hardware store and a Purity supermarket—welcomed Woolworth's as one of its own.

Woolworth's was one of the original stores when the Stanford Shopping Center opened in 1955.
[THE CAROLYN PIERCE POSTCARD COLLECTION]

By the 1980s, however, the Stanford Shopping Center had experienced some serious upward mobility. While Woolworth's was still a profitable store and the ideal place to pick up some AA batteries, low-priced shampoo or a pack of gum, its general merchandise had increasingly become an anathema to the Stanford Shopping Center's new market strategy. In 1986, Rosemary McAndrews, the overseer of Stanford's march to boutiqueville, said that Woolworth's no longer "fit the Stanford image." Indeed, Woolworth's did seem a bit out of place alongside Tiffany's, Bloomingdale's and Pottery Barn for Kids.

Actually, by the 1990s Woolworth's was struggling all over the country. Its market niche had been usurped by the bigger all-purpose stores like Walmart and Target which offered more brands, more square footage and a lot more parking. Additionally, as supermarkets and drug stores expanded to sell more than just food and medicine, Woolworth's value declined.

In 1994, Woolworth's closed more than half of its 800 locations across the nation, but Palo Alto's two stores were already gone. The Woolworth's on University Avenue made its final sale in 1989, and the Stanford Shopping Center Woolworth's bowed to pressure in 1991. The glory days were surely over for the once mighty Woolworth's—so completely over that six years later, consolidating its retail assets, the Woolworth Corporation made the decision to change its name to the Venator Group. The name Woolworth's, it seemed, was just so yesterday.

The closing of the Woolworth's at the Stanford Shopping Center in 1991.

Postcard showing the bar at L'Omelette—a president's old stomping grounds. [THE CAROLYN PIERCE POSTCARD COLLECTION]

RESTAURANT ROW
Some Good Ol' Palo Alto Cooking

S ET OUT ON ANY MAJOR AMERICAN HIGHWAY THESE DAYS AND YOUR CHOICES FOR LUNCH are pretty limited. Unless you want to forego making "good time," your roadside options usually consist of six fast food logos arranged neatly on a blue "Gas Food Lodging" sign. And with rare exception the choices do not stray very far from some combination of Taco Bell, McDonalds, KFC, and the like. Down South you may find a few more Hardee's and out here you might see an In-N-Out or two, but a highway lunch is going to pretty much consist of something deep fried and coming through your car window in a white paper bag.

But there was a time when the eating possibilities on the American roadway were an essential part of what it meant to travel, when the array of cuisines and restaurants that each community offered was part of the tapestry of the trip. Back then the roads most travelled were not anonymous interstates but distinctive state highways, and the landscape was dotted with fancy restaurants, rickety old hot dog stands and occasionally a diamond in the roadside rough.

A postcard of Rickey's in a far less developed South Palo Alto. [THE CAROLYN PIERCE POSTCARD COLLECTION]

After World War II and well into the 1970s, El Camino Real in Palo Alto was one of those highways. As old US 101, El Camino was a main road leading from San Francisco to San Jose—as such, it was a kind of showcase for restaurants vying to fill the stomachs of hungry travelers.

The stretch of El Camino in southern Palo Alto was a popular locale for restaurants wishing to avoid strict liquor laws. State laws passed after Prohibition banned hard alcohol sales within a mile and a half of college campuses such as Stanford. As a result, dinner couples, travelers and university students in search of a drink frequented Restaurant Row on the old King's Highway.

Three of the most storied of these restaurants were owned at one time by the same man— the venerable restaurateur and hotel wiz, John Rickey. Rickey's Studio Inn, Rick's Swiss Chalet

An ad encouraging Rickey's Studio Club patrons to "net a big one." [THE CAROLYN PIERCE POSTCARD COLLECTION]

and Dinah's Shack (bought by Rickey in 1950) were all well-known stops for Highway 101 travelers. And they demonstrated the great variety of cuisines that could be found on one road.

Dinah's Shack began in the late '20s as a Southern style chicken-on-toast stand—to which Rickey later added the scores of appetizers to be found in the famed Scandinavian smorgasbord. Rick's Swiss Chalet was geared specifically to the food and tastes of the owner's native Switzerland and provided European ambiance, courtesy of Southern Bavaria's Edelweiss Trio. The Chalet hosted the first meeting of the still-active Peninsula Swiss Club. From 1961-1985, the restaurant served some 3 million meals on El Camino Way where the Goodwill store now stands.

Rickey's Studio Club became a local hot spot in the 1950s and for more reasons than just Mrs. Rickey's secret-recipe cheesecake. The cuisine was admired in the northern part of the state and its dining room featured paintings from Rickey's vast (and rather expensive) art collection.

Other options along Restaurant Row provided international flavors from all over the world. Chinese Chicken Salad and other tastes of the Orient could be found at Ming's Chinese Restaurant at the corner of El Camino and Vista Road (Ming's moved to its current location off Embarcadero Road in 1967). Fine French cuisine thrived just off El Camino at Villa Lafayette—home to chef Adrien Jouan, who had started cooking as a 10-year-old apprentice in Paris.

In 1956, brothers Harry, Rudy, George and Art Alfinito opened the beloved Rudolpho's at the corner of Los Robles Avenue and El Camino. The brothers would spend more than three decades serving cannelloni to Jimmy Durante and other not-so-famous clientele at their distinctive red-checkered tables. In 1993, the restaurant was closed and later bulldozed to make way for apartments after the City Council changed the zoning status of the block—a controversial action that brought angry protests from spaghetti fans all over Barron Park.

Aside from fine dining, Restaurant Row provided Palo Alto with its share of the 1950s drive-in experience, forever memorialized nationally in "American Graffiti" and "Happy Days." Restaurant Row had a number of drive-ins including the John Barnes Drive-In, the Carousel and Bonander's—as well as an A&W franchise. After its move from Middlefield Road, the A&W became a rare chain eatery along the largely independently-owned Restaurant Row.

The drive-ins were, of course, a prime hangout for teenagers before the days of big indoor malls. Slicked-back boys and their poodle-skirted dates would pull up at parking stalls fitted with speakers to order Mama or Papa Burgers, Chili Dogs and 11-cent French fries. Brightly attired carhops zipped out the food, allowing the kids to remain in their car to eat "on the drive." Indeed, this was the beginning of the drive-in era which included the popular practice which seems a bit odd these days—watching a full-length movie from a vantage point behind your windshield.

Of course, the drive-in restaurants tended to attract a different crowd from the sit-down options along Restaurant Row. While the Rickey's restaurants generally appealed to travelling families or those in search of a martini with dinner, the drive-ins attracted high school locals. In 1966, the A&W which stood at 4127 El Camino Real (the current site of the Tofu House) became the subject of City Council inquiries when neighbors complained of drunken rowdiness, burning rubber and "uncontrolled pandemonium." A police crackdown quieted down the kids but also brought some 31 citations in less than a month.

A drive-in restaurant along El Camino, 1950s.

While there have been some independent success stories during the past few decades, including Hobee's ("home of the famous coffeecake") and Jose's Caribbean Restaurant (which advertised their "worst pizza in town"), the old legends of Restaurant Row are long gone. They were the victims of a number of changes—competition from the chic restaurants that have thrived downtown since liquor laws were lifted, the diversion of travelers to Bayshore Freeway, zoning changes and an abundance of fast-food drive-thrus which further serve a culture "on the drive."

The last of the great old restaurants of Restaurant Row came down in 1995. It was known for years as L'Omelette, a cozy, wood-paneled restaurant that looked something like a French farmhouse. Legend has it that in 1940, Jack Kennedy, while on a brief stint at Stanford Business School, held court at a certain L'Ommies barstool surrounded by a regular throng of groupies.

Having thrived through the '50s and '60s, L'Omelette stumbled during the '70s until French chef Louis Borel took it over, revived it, and in 1981 renamed it Chez Louis. There he entertained the likes of Joan Baez, Bill Walsh and Hewlett and Packard. But after 20 years, the old master could no longer compete with downtown and the chain restaurants that had closed in on him. As Borel told the *San Francisco Chronicle* with a tear, "It doesn't fit. You can't make it fit. It is a restaurant from another era." In 1995, the old place finally came down, bulldozed to make way for the Walgreen's that stands there now. For Restaurant Row, it was the last supper, as time—and California's highway travelers—had long passed it by.

Jose liked to claim he had the "Worst Pizza in Town."

An abandoned Peninsula Creamery truck in a Palo Alto back alley, circa 1970.

A DELIVERY FROM THE PAST
Palo Alto's Milkmen

"Where did the milkman go?" ask Susan Jonas and Marilyn Nissenson in their wonderful 1994 book, *Going, Going, Gone*. The authors answer that question in a collection of articles describing "Vanishing Americana"—artifacts and habits we think of as quintessentially American, but which are no longer with us. Some of the items are interesting to remember but have few supporters rallying for their return—rotary phones, girdles and leisure suits come to mind. But then there are those cherished slices of Americana that still hold a place in the nation's collective memory. Bike-riding paperboys, doctors who make house calls and gas station attendants who check your oil and tires no longer make much business sense. Still, when they faded away, it seemed that some part of the American community left with them.

And what about the milkman? The memory of the driver stepping out of the Divco truck in his crisp white suit to drop off those glass bottles—is there anything that seems both so outdated and yet so sadly lost?

After all, these days it is possible to run your daily errands with an almost total lack of social interaction. You can pump self-service gas, shop at the grocery store (an increasing number have self-checkouts), bank at the ATM (avoiding the teller fees) and even end up at an automated post office machine—all without ever speaking to a live person. And when you do interact with a salesperson or clerk, it is often a cold, machine-like transaction. Not that you can really blame the person behind the counter. Sure, maybe a trip to family-operated establishments like J J & F's Market or Bell's Books will get you a big how-do-you-do and some personal service. But it's hard to fault the underpaid and often under-respected workers at the big national chain stores if they start to view you as just one of hundreds of transactions in an eight-hour shift.

The Peninsula Creamery Dairy Store at 900 High Street is still run by the Santana family.
[PHOTO: MATT BOWLING]

In days past, the milkman was perhaps the ultimate illustration of customer service. Originally, poor refrigeration meant that milk was delivered daily with the aid of horses that knew the routes by heart, stopping at each house while their bosses carried the crates of glass bottles to the doorstep. Hence the phrase, "Change the milkman but not the horse." Even in the Great Depression, 70% of milk sold was delivered door-to-door by more than 70,000 milkmen nationwide.

Milkmen were always more than just deliverymen with dairy products. Many kept a house key and put the milk, eggs and cheese right in the refrigerator—or, in the early days, down in a cellar ice box. They were also known to help in other ways—leaving food out for a dog or cat, reaching something on a high shelf for an elderly customer, changing a fuse for an ill-equipped housewife. And many old-timers still remember the yellowish cream at the top of the bottle that on cold days would expand outside into "high hats," and the endless vaudeville jokes about the milkman's good fortune at spending the workday visiting lonely housewives from 9 to 5.

From its early days, Palo Alto was a kind of regional dairy capital. As far back as 1906, local milk was sent to San Francisco following the earthquake. A 1930 *Palo Alto Times* story tells with pride of three Palo Alto dairies that finished "win, place and show" at the Pacific Slope Dairy Show in Oakland. Indeed, in the first half of the 20th century, creamery plants and soda fountains thrived in Palo Alto. Piers Dairy, the Golden State Creamery, Easton Creamery, Altamont Creamery, University Creamery, and Gold Seal Creamery all did brisk business.

Most successful of all was the Peninsula Creamery, whose milkmen at one point served some 12,000 customers in their red-and-cream colored trucks. Founded in 1922 by Axel Raven and Howard Cobb, the boys soon established a brand name and slogan—"Made right, right in Palo Alto"—mostly through ambition, a 3 a.m. daily wake-up time, eight-cent milk pints and a rented Ford truck. In 1936, the Creamery was bought by John Santana, who turned the Peninsula Creamery fountain on Emerson Street into a local institution by selling "Choc Malts," BLTs and the thickest shakes in town to travelers and Paly students alike.

The old Peninsula Creamery fountain (top) on Emerson is now officially the Palo Alto Creamery (bottom). Although its sign doesn't reflect the change, it is no longer run by the Santanas. [PHOTO: MATT BOWLING]

Milk delivered from the Peninsula Creamery plant was different from the dairy products available at the newfangled supermarkets. A 1950s' ad told of the "extra freshness" that came from producing milk from the 700 or so cows on "our Peninsula Troutmere Guernsey Farm, thereby assuring fresh pure wholesome milk." Originally Creamery cows had roamed the Stanford pastures where the Stanford Shopping Center now stands.

Ice cream was an even bigger seller. From 1957 to 1994, the Peninsula Creamery plant turned out as much as three million gallons a year and more than 200 flavors. The well-known label could also be found in Bay Area supermarkets. Still, despite its popularity, the Creamery shut down its milk bottling plant in 1985. The ice cream plant lasted until 1994, when a city directive to switch from an ammonia coolant system to Freon proved too expensive.

Of course, milkmen had met their demise in the Bay Area even earlier. By the 1960s most folks were picking up their dairy products on trips to Safeway or Lucky. And although Creamery milkmen hung around until the 1980s, eventually even they faded away.

And yet there is still one milkman in Palo Alto who keeps the tradition alive. For 21 years, "Michal the Milkman" has been delivering milk, cheese, butter, cream—even Choco Tacos and Astropops. When the Palo Alto native started his business in 1987, with fond memories of Wally, the Peninsula Creamery milkman of his childhood days, Michal had so few deliveries he carried them in a backpack on his Yamaha motorcycle. But word soon spread about this milkman survivor, and his customer base grew. Today he and his crew of milkmen deliver to nearly 200 loyalists, big and small, in a vintage fleet of trucks from the '60s, '50s and even '40s.

Like his milkmen forefathers, Michal does more than deliver dairy products. Some customers give him their house keys so he can put the milk right in the fridge, and he has been known to do small household chores for older folks. A few years back, one 93-year-old customer fell. Rather than use his emergency button, he simply waited for Michal to arrive the next day to help him up. Another time the milkman found a high-schooler in tux and tails whose prom ride had fallen through. Soon he was standing on the floorboard of Michal's milk truck, setting a new standard for arriving at the prom in style. For many customers, Michal is like one of the family—and as such he is rewarded with thank-you notes, cookies, children's drawings, even Beanie Babies.

Today Michal is on the internet at *Michalthemilkman.com*, but his style remains easygoing and personable. One website blog entry updates customers that "Georgie caught a flat off Greer a few minutes ago. The tire guy is on the way for a roadside repair and we expect to be back on the route in about an hour." And in the website's testimonials section, there is an evaluation from 5-year-old Jimmy, "I like Michal. He's nice. He got my ball out of the tree."

And isn't that the legacy of the milkman? A delivery man and a dairy salesman, to be sure—but also, a friend who gets your ball out of the tree.

Top: A Michal the Milkman driver pulls up for a delivery, 2012. Bottom: A milkman with two children.
[PHOTOS: MICHAL THE MILKMAN]

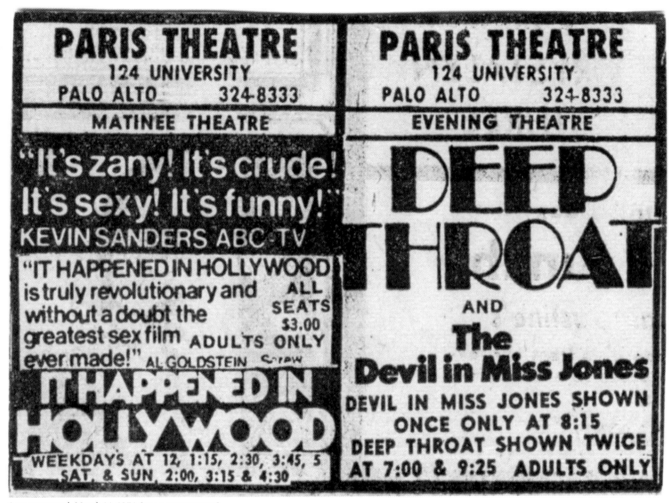

A newspaper ad, March 14, 1974. [PALO ALTO TIMES]

THE PARIS THEATRE
Prurience or Porno-Chic?

UNIVERSITY AVENUE HAS CHANGED A GREAT DEAL OVER THE PAST 30 YEARS, AND PERHAPS nothing illustrates that transformation as much as the story of the Paris Theatre. The X-rated movie house operated during the 1970s at 124 University Avenue, near Alma Street and the Circle, giving Palo Alto a rather unseemly entry point to the downtown area. During its time as the city's most visible adult theatre, the Paris brought local context to the national debate over obscenity. While the nation's high court grappled with what constituted "obscene" and what was protected under the First Amendment, Palo Altans struggled with what was permissible according to their own community's standards. As sexual mores changed during the 1960s, X-rated movie houses, increasingly explicit girly magazines and strip clubs challenged the nation's legal system to define exactly what constituted obscenity in a changing society. But definitions would not come easy. Using phrases like "utterly without redeeming social value," the Supreme Court seemed only to muddle the issue for the public and law enforcement. And porn producers were quick to circumvent High Court definitions with tricks such as slipping in passages of Shakespeare to add a little civility to otherwise carnal proceedings. Legal confusion meant that term after term, dirty books, movies, and magazines kept ending up back in the lap of the nation's highest court, which presumably had more important business to attend to.

The court wound up making obscenity law even less clear when Justice Potter Stewart refused to define hard-core pornography, stating in his 1964 opinion for Jacobellis v. Ohio, "I shall not today attempt further to define [what is obscene] ... but I know it when I see it." Without any meaningful definition, the High Court was in the position of potentially ruling on virtually every obscenity arrest made for showing porn films all across the country. This led to somewhat

Justice Potter Stewart who famously said of obscenity: "I know it when I see it." [WIKIPEDIA COMMONS/LIBRARY OF CONGRESS/OAKES, 1976]

ridiculous "movie days," in which the Supreme Court clerks joined the all-male, largely octogenarian body to eat popcorn and watch the porn movies from cases awaiting decisions.

Eventually, the court essentially gave up on such specific review, giving far more general instructions on obscenity in 1973's Miller v. California—guidelines that more or less still stand. In that case the court said that judges must look at whether the "average person, applying contemporary community standards, would find that the work, taken as a whole, appeals to the prurient interest." But of course, even that mouthful was subject to vastly different interpretations.

As obscenity rules loosened, pornography reached its own golden age. The porn films of the 1970s added a touch of art which allowed them to gain further acceptance in mainstream society. The feature film "Deep Throat" was released in 1972, and its stunning popularity helped usher in a new look at pornography. It was the beginning of what has been called porno-chic. Soon a series of other films tried to blend artistic sophistication with hard-core sex. As '70s porn director Ron Wertheim said, "I approached those films as if I was Luc Godard or somebody." For a time in urban areas, it even became trendy for younger moviegoers to attend porn films. Major newspapers like the *New York Times* and *Chicago Sun-Times* and magazines like *Time* and *Newsweek* began reviewing some soft-core and even hard-core movies, and many in the industry believed that the adult genre would soon blend into mainstream Hollywood.

And of course before the age of VCRs, hotel pay-per-view and the all-time heavyweight of porn content—the internet—X-rated movie houses were the primary places where those with the aforementioned "prurient interests" could satisfy their curiosities. In the 1970s it seemed that most cities had at least one local theatre showing dirty movies. In Palo Alto, that place was the Paris Theatre, and the fact that it was right on University Avenue rankled many in town.

Opening in 1961, the Paris Theatre originally showed artsy American indies and foreign films like its opener, Jean Renoir's "Picnic on the Grass." But as profits began to sink and porno-chic took off, the double bills at the Paris became adult-only affairs. By the early '70s the Paris was showing such X-rated films as "Ginger" ("her weapon is her body") and "The School Girls," which promised to be "an intimate study of the hidden lives of our teen-age girls—shocking, revealing, true!"

After the Supreme Court's decision in Miller in 1973, the Paris Theatre became a target of the local PAPD. On September 21 of that year, police raided the Paris and seized its copy of "The Devil in Miss Jones," one of the all-time pieces of artsy filth. Police Chief James Zurcher told the

An ad for "The School Girls" playing at the Paris Theatre. [PALO ALTO TIMES]

press that "based on recently decided cases, it's apparent that exhibiting a film such as 'The Devil in Miss Jones' is unlawful" and he had a warrant to verify the point. Still, no arrests were made and the owners, San Carlos Cinema Inc., didn't seem too worried about it. They quickly obtained another copy and continued showing the film for the rest of its scheduled run at the theatre.

Three months later the police were back to nab the theatre's copy of "Deep Throat," which officers said violated Penal Code Section 311.2—distributing, exhibiting or advertising obscene material. Police seemed defensive about such morality arrests, however, noting that they did not have "a detail that worries about pornography" and that "it is very low on our list of priorities."

Strangely, in 1976 Paris owner, Hal Snyder picketed his own theatre. He claimed that Santa Clara County Superior Court Judge Edward Brady had executed the lease with San Carlos Cinema over his objections during a divorce action from his wife, Adrienne. Few details were given, but he showed up with his 14- and 12-year-old sons who Snyder said had been teased at school. They marched with signs saying, "The courts put porno in my dad's show—then kids drove me from school."

By the summer of 1977, the City Council was looking to relocate the Paris Theatre. Councilman Alan Henderson floated the idea of the Paris switching locations with the family-oriented Biograph Theatre on more secluded Ramona Street or the funky Festival Cinema on Hamilton. San Carlos Cinema, who seemed to want to get out of the line of fire from increasingly hostile Palo Alto residents, supported the move. One such resident, Pete Norway of the Concerned Citizens Group, objected to the move saying "we should not encourage [the Paris] to stay in our city."

Then, in December of 1977, discussion halted when the theatre owners decided to close the Paris. They cited the deteriorating condition of the theatre, although it seems community pressure was also a major factor. Eventually the Paris was sold for $510,000 and was remodeled for retail. Today, the rather sterile E-Trade Financial stands at the former home of Palo Alto's memorable venture into the golden age of porn.

These days, adult films in the United States generate some $20 billion in revenues and constitute two-thirds of all hotel movie purchases. As porn has continued to grow in America, it has also gone back underground. Secreted pay-per-view movies and private internet surfing have replaced the gaudy exhibitionism and flashing lights of the old X-rated theatres. And these days in Palo Alto, any chic exhibited on University Avenue is strictly confined to shoes and skirts.

The Paris Theatre in 1976 with owner Hal Snyder and his two sons picketing his own theatre. [PALO ALTO TIMES/JOE MELENA]

Palo Alto boys ride their decorated bicycles in a 1941 parade on University Avenue.

BIKES IN PALO ALTO
A Ride Through History

There is a reminiscent scene that takes place in Palo Alto each afternoon that seems more 1950s than present day. Waiting at the light at Newell and Embarcadero any weekday around 3 PM, you'll see a crossing guard stop the busy flow of cars as a swarm of kids bike home from Jordan Middle School. It's been a similar sight for decades as boys and girls trade jokes and gossip while balancing books, lunch bags and backpacks on their ride home to the neighborhood. Still, despite this visual throwback, bicycles are not as central to this generation. There was a time when the bicycle was more important in the life of a Palo Alto child than a TV, Xbox or cell phone is today. For kids of that earlier era, the bicycle meant freedom.

Childhood memories of those who grew up in Palo Alto often revolve around the bicycle. Up through the '40s, '50s and '60s, bikes were indispensable to kids from the time the training wheels came off until they got their first driver's license. It was a different era—a time of independence and innocence in which parents were not in the business of shuttling their children from "playdates" to soccer practice and back home again. The bike offered school-age riders a sense of freedom—a chance to explore their surroundings, visit friends and, of course, get into mischief.

Combing through the memories of grown-up Palo Altans on the local Town Square Forum, virtually every recollection of the halcyon days of youth has to do with a bicycle. Forum posters remember "Riding bikes down the dry creek beds" and "Riding our bikes to the 'drive-up' window at Berkeley Farms for snow-cones." One poster memorably describes "Sneaking across Middlefield on our bikes to buy candy and gum at Fran's on Lytton Street. I remember my little brother, Perry, and his friends constantly getting in trouble for playing in the creek. The evidence was usually poison oak rashes and/or yet another lost bike."

Mayfielders in the late 1880s on old penny farthings.
[PALO ALTO HISTORICAL ASSOCIATION/W. H. MYRICK]

Kids in the 1950s park their bikes at the Junior Museum.

A Palo Alto mailman using a bicycle to deliver mail.

In those days parents were not seen as derelict in allowing their kids to roam the neighborhoods on their bikes. Perhaps there was less danger or perhaps those dangers just weren't so publicized. Either way, kids had more space back then. One Palo Altan remembered "Riding bikes all over town without parents knowing where we were—no problem." Another recalled, "Riding bikes and skateboards all over town all summer and no one worried," while a third recollected "Never fearing anything and always feeling safe and secure riding our bikes and playing on a warm summer evening."

Not that the hordes of kids on bikes in town didn't present a few problems. The old Palo Alto papers are full of stories of city higher-ups trying to deal with kids and bikes. For instance, youngsters going to the movies had a habit of just throwing their bikes into piles on the city sidewalk. Of course, this troubled the window shoppers on University Avenue who had a tendency to trip over them. It seemed shop owners were in a constant losing battle to keep their front entrances clear of stray bikes. In 1947, Police Chief Howard Zink caused his share of grief enforcing an ordinance that prohibited obstruction of the sidewalk by bicycles. After impounding 22 bikes on the first day, Zink was besieged with kids at Police Court with "tearful and vociferous protests" according to the *Palo Alto Times*.

It was a similar scene in the 1950s when the Council tried to enforce license plates on the city's estimated 13,000 bikes. A license could be had by passing a short test and paying a dollar. This measure was in response to the remarkable amount of bicycles being stolen—some 80 bikes in a single month in 1948. It seems that for many kids, bikes were virtually communal property. Someone took your bike last week, maybe you borrow one this week. There were also attempts to educate young riders to be more aware of traffic laws, although such efforts could sometimes come across as a bit heavy-handed. One 1941 city pamphlet for young bike riders begins with the somewhat overbearing statement that "Riding a bicycle on the streets and highways is a privilege granted us by the city and state free of charge."

Bike contests and parades were also popular in Palo Alto both before and after the war. For instance, a 1940 Bicycle Day at Rinconada Park included "three-way relays, obstacle races, stunts and elegant prizes for riders with decorated bicycles." There was a "Cycle Trade of America Silver Cup Trophy" to shoot for and a plank ride in which boys and girls tried to ride their bikes across a wooden plank that was 150 feet long, five inches wide, and one inch thick. One year Eddie

Hill made it all the way across three times in a row. In Palo Alto's earliest days, however, bike contests weren't just for the kids. In the late 1880s, the modern bicycle was invented and those high-wheeled penny-farthings were put in the back of the shed. The new faster, safer bikes soon produced bicycle clubs all across the country. On the Peninsula, biking was near fanatical. As proof, look no farther than the popular "Century Race," a 100-mile, ten-hour jaunt from San Jose, up the East Bay, across a ferry and back down the Peninsula. Fanaticism went a bit too far during one San Jose race when a rival club member shot biker Emil Agraz in the ankle with seven miles to go—somehow Emil still managed to win his group.

Indeed, San Jose was biking central as the famed Garden City Wheelmen and other top clubs turned out Olympic riders and national cycling champion Otto Zeilger Jr., known as "The Little Demon." Later San Jose became the first and last city in the United States to own its own velodrome, a cycling-only stadium.

But young Palo Alto was also home to a devoted group of cyclists with competitive teams such as the Mayfield Wheelmen and the Palo Alto Cycle Club. A further highlight each year was the "businessman's invitation race" in which local merchants competed. The *Palo Alto Times* reported in 1895 on one such Saturday morning contest. The finish was described with great pizzazz. Lumberman, bank president and future mayor J.F. Parkinson "came down the avenue amid great shouts and turned the corner onto Alma Street with a sweep that nearly took their breath away and caused a cloud of dust to follow…like that which follows the flyer. Parkinson was in the lead pulling out for the win, his light coat fanning the breeze like a mizzen sail." Clearly if the so-called "Father of Palo Alto" could ride like that, bicycles and the city would long be linked.

And indeed they have been. Now more than a century later, Palo Alto's longtime fondness for the bicycle remains. The city's friendly attitude toward cyclists is still evident in its 30 miles of bike lanes, the Bryant Street Bicycle Boulevard (the nation's first such enterprise) and popular bike trails to be scouted out at the Palo Alto Baylands. In May 2003, Palo Alto became one of just four cities nationwide to be named as a gold-level "Bicycle Friendly Community" by the League of American Bicyclists. So while kids today may not ride all over town like previous generations, Palo Alto has not lost its love for what the old-timers simply called "The Wheel." It seems it has been in our blood ever since old Mr. Parkinson set out in his cloud of dust.

Sign marking Bryant Street Bicycle Boulevard, 2012.
[PHOTO: BRIAN GEORGE]

Cubberley school spirit in the 1960s

THE CUBBERLEY CLOSING
A Tough Call

Sometimes in politics it seems that you just can't win. No matter what's decided, somebody's going home unhappy. In 1979, the Palo Alto Unified School District Board faced such a political Catch-22. There were three high schools in town and one of them was going to have to close—and it was pretty clear that whichever school was shut down would have a lot of angry parents, students and staff members holding a serious grudge.

A combination of factors saddled the School Board with such an unpalatable choice. The first was the 1978 statewide passage of the mother of all ballot initiatives—Proposition 13. While the enactment of this "taxpayer's revolt" reduced property taxes, it also put wealthier school districts like PAUSD on precarious financial footing. No longer able to rely on the affluent local tax base, the district was $2 million in the red by 1979.

At the same time that the district was hemorrhaging money, it was also losing students. By 1979, Palo Alto had nearly a thousand fewer students than in 1973, as enrollment plummeted 30 percent between 1967 and 1979.

To Superintendent Newman Walker, these factors led to an obvious conclusion—one high school and a number of elementary schools would have to be closed. Walker argued that Cubberley would have to be that high school. The argument went like this: Palo Alto Senior High School (a.k.a. "Paly") and Henry M. Gunn High School were both on Stanford land. Walker reported to the School Board that if these schools closed, the land would revert to Stanford for the original price—$358,000 in the case of Gunn and just $26,000 in the case of Paly, which opened in 1918.

That argument carried the day, as the School Board salivated over the $11 million that Walker said Cubberley's 35 acres might fetch. On February 6, 1979, in front of 600 persons and numerous

The Cubberley student body officers for the 1969–70 school year. They are Debbie Hill, Jerry Macklin, Pam Sawyer and Chris Fleming.

Cubberley grads on the final day, June 14, 1979.
[PALO ALTO TIMES TRIBUNE]

television crews at Paly's auditorium, the School Board voted 3-2 to shut down Cubberley at the end of the school year.

However, things turned out to be a little more complicated than Walker had suggested. The Superintendent had to backtrack on a key point: money obtained from a sale of Cubberley could only be put in the District's general fund if the land were sold to a non-profit or public agency, otherwise the money would have to be used for far more limited "capital expenditures."

Now Cubberley defenders saw an opportunity to make their case: Cubberley had a higher enrollment capacity than Gunn, a larger cafeteria and the only equipped space to house classes for the acoustically handicapped and the educable mentally disabled. They also pointed out that Cubberley had been around longer and had a more dynamic reputation as a school of innovation and excellence. And both Cubberley and Gunn supporters argued that their school was actually closer to the home of the average Palo Alto high schooler.

Debate persisted even as Cubberley's final graduates prepared to receive their diplomas in June. Supporters of Cubberley formed a group called Take Time to Plan which maintained that the District should reconsider closing any high schools. They collected more than 6,000 signatures of those agreeing that the closure decision be put to a citywide vote.

Take Time to Plan also took their fight to the courts and on March 30th convinced Santa Clara County Superior Court Judge Stanley Evans that the School Board's action was subject to voter referendum. The district was now faced with three choices: appeal the decision, rescind the Cubberley closure, or put the whole question up for a costly and divisive citywide election. No one was shocked when they decided to appeal.

They made the right move. On May 30th, 1979, the California Court of Appeals overturned Judge Evans in a 3-0 ruling, siding with the School District and maintaining that School Board decisions were administrative, not legislative. The fight to save Cubberley was effectively lost.

As emotions calmed and students moved on, the School Board's decision gained respect. In the fall of the 1979, 950 former Cubberley students reported to school at either Gunn or Paly with a minimum of disruption. Meanwhile, the old high school became the Cubberley Community Center which still exists today. Perhaps in the end the School Board's decision to close Cubberley was actually a political winner—it just took a couple of decades to find out.

CONFLICTS

A look down Bryant Street when trees stood in the street, circa 1910.

SAVE THE OAKS!
Palo Alto's First Environmental Victory

IN THE 20TH CENTURY URBAN ENVIRONMENTS WERE OVERHAULED TO SUIT THE AUTOmobile. As the early "horseless carriage"—a novelty toy for the rich—was transformed into an essential appliance of the American Dream, the environment changed to accommodate this new way of life. In the 1920s, new roads and highways crisscrossed the country linking small towns and large cities. In the 1950s, the interstate highway system sent freeways and turnpikes over farmland, across pastoral vistas, and over (and sometimes through) mountain ranges.

In the 1960s and '70s, highways headed for downtown, often dividing urban neighborhoods right down the middle, forcing out tenants and homeowners through the power of eminent domain. And urban main streets became increasingly suited to the automobile. Parking lots, endless strip malls (with acres of convenient parking), and six and eight lane boulevards were built to deal with ever-worsening urban traffic and parking problems. Today, cities like Los Angeles are now virtually enemy territory for pedestrians who are often forced to walk downtown in elevated walkways connecting office buildings. Even in a smaller city like Palo Alto, crossing a car-friendly "traffic artery" like El Camino Real is no treat.

Not that there haven't been those who have tried to stop the ever-expanding empire of the automobile. Locally, former Mayor Yoriko Kishimoto has been a consistent supporter of the concept of the "walkable city," backing shuttles, bike lanes, farmers' markets and even favoring temporary day-long conversions of University Avenue to a pedestrian plaza.

But Palo Alto's first environmentalists to fight automobile dominance were those who battled to "Save the Oaks" in 1914. These were early days for the automobile, just six years after Henry Ford's first Model T "put America on wheels." Still, there were already some 225 automobiles in

An ad for saving the oaks instructs how to mark the ballot in the 1914 election.

the Palo Alto area, zigging and zagging through city streets avoiding horses, carriages, pedestrians and sometimes trees.

Indeed, if the car now reigns supreme in American culture, it didn't even have the roadway to itself in 1914. Some 132 oak trees stood in 25 Palo Alto streets, often right in the center of the road. Bryant Street had 11 oaks in just 12 blocks and 13 oaks stood in Cowper Street over a 13-block distance. Since horse-drawn buggies had little difficulty navigating the occasional road-blocking tree, Palo Alto's original street grids simply let the trees stand as they had for hundreds of years.

But cars and trees did not share the road so easily. Without street lights, warning signs, or windshield wipers, drivers in unfavorable conditions had a tendency to run headlong into these beautiful old oaks. This was the case in early 1914 when Dr. Benjamin Thomas smashed head-on into a Bryant Street oak, creating an eight-inch gash in the mature tree. He claimed that city officials were negligent for allowing such a dangerous object to remain in the street and sued for $5,000. Although he eventually lost, during the progression of the case through the courts, Palo Alto's City Council considered handing over the streets to the automobile permanently. Many feared that more injuries and lawsuits lay ahead if the trees remained. Sure enough, Palo Alto Councilman George Mosher drove his car into a tree during the months that the Council was considering the issue and later that year Mrs. H. J. Moule slammed into the same tree as Dr. Thomas. In fact, the *Palo Alto Times* reported in 1915, rather incredibly, that a dozen cars crashed into that one tree over a two-year period, making one wonder if the tree didn't have some sort of otherworldly magnetic pull.

Debate was heated on both sides of the tree question. Palo Alto's noted environmental sensibilities were apparent even in this era in the assertions that the trees should remain. One woman pleaded to Palo Altans in a *Times* op-ed to "Save their lives! With what infinite patience have they persisted through the stress of many years, offering protection to man and beast with arms continuously outstretched in love and benediction to all. No, you cannot take the life of such friends and benefactors."

Some even felt that the threat of a dangerous tree lurking down a dark street could be a beneficial incentive for drivers to slow down. Several hundred school children signed a petition to the

Long-time council member George Mosher crashed into a street tree in 1915.

City Council to spare the oaks and one advocate wrote dreamily of twin trees on Cowper Street, "a Gothic arch…shaped perfectly by the Creator's hand… and placed at the gateway to our city."

But others believed that the center-lane trees were an obstacle to progress, including nine out of fifteen City Council members. In an 1,100 word leaflet distributed to some 1,500 Palo Altans, Councilman E. A. Hettinger argued in favor of his proposal to remove any oak standing within the "driveway part of any street from gutter to gutter." He then placed a rather heavy burden on the voters, warning that "if you cast your vote to leave these obstructions to jeopardize life and property—these perilous monuments to sentiment—and a life is lost, your conscience must be your accuser for you have voluntarily shared in the blame."

Another advocate, I. A. Fickel, perhaps more reasonably contended that "The auto has come to stay and its increase in the next 10 years will be marvelous… we have got to adjust ourselves to a faster life… every means must be used to keep the roadway clear of obstructions."

On September 11, 1914, Palo Alto voters went to the polls to decide the fate of the trees. They soundly defeated the Hettinger plan to eliminate all street trees by a vote of 528–308. The fate of each tree was then to be determined by the Council individually, resulting in many trees later being "whitewashed" near their base to make them easier to see on a dark night. Today you can still find an occasional whitewashed tree in Palo Alto.

Of course, in the end the trees were fighting a hopeless battle against the revving engines of modernity. Little by little, the oaks were brought down, clearing the way for the automobile to dominate the center of both the road and American society.

A tree remains on Cowper Street across from the former Kathleen Norris house. [PHOTO: MATT BOWLING]

Anti-Negro incidents rapped by Zink, Doyle

PALO ALTO TIMES
AUG 7 '51

Palo Alto's chief of police and police judge today struck out against persons responsible for a pair of anti-Negro incidents reported last week.

Friday the Jerusalem Baptist Church at 398 Sheridan Ave. reported that "KKK" had been painted in red letters seven inches high on its sidewalk.

Earlier, Mrs. Helen Wright, operator of a restaurant at 1705 El Camino Real, complained of receiving a note saying, "Your last warning. The Black Ace."

Said Police Chief Howard A. Zink:

"I feel very definitely that Palo Alto of all cities should be above that sort of thing and serve as a model for other cities. It seems that we have certain people in this city who do not recognize that responsibility.

"With our educational advantages, we should have sufficient tolerance to understand that there is no superior race.

"Our people have an obligation to do everything in their power to show that we stand for complete understanding and tolerance of other races.

"In America, with our constitution and our background, we are in a very poor position if we allow this sort of thing to appear while we are in the role of world leadership."

Police Judge Richard E. Doyle Jr. said "It's a shame something like this has to happen in Palo Alto."

He recalled that several years ago another KKK was painted on the pavement at Homer Ave. and Ramona St.

"I don't know of any such organization here, and I certainly hope that the incidents are the work of pranksters, and not serious threats."

Aug. 7, 1951 [PALO ALTO TIMES]

THE KKK IN PALO ALTO
Terror vs Tolerance

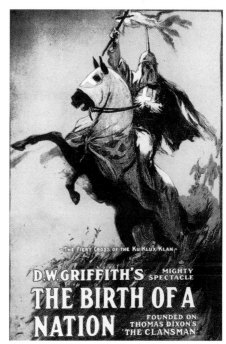

The poster for the film, "The Birth of a Nation," which resurrected interest in the Klan. [WIKIPEDIA COMMONS/CHRONICLE OF THE CINEMA, 1915]

BEFORE THE ADVENT OF MOVIES, RADIO, AND TELEVISION, OUR COUNTRY WAS MORE dispersed in a psychological sense. The mass media has given Americans a shared culture, a common reference point. In our history shared experiences have brought the country together—watching men walk on the moon, listening to Fireside Chats, cheering on Olympians. But the mass media has also been used to rally hate and intolerance—McCarthyism, George Wallace. One of the earliest and most despicable cultural phenomena driven by the mass media was the rise of the Ku Klux Klan. Before radio or TV, the silent movie was the nation's most important cultural media experience and a 1915 film would prove just how important the movies could be.

Although the Klan had its first life in the years following the Civil War, the KKK basically died out with the end of Reconstruction. Years later, the resurrection of the Klan was inspired by D. W. Griffith's "Birth of a Nation," a three-hour film based on Rev. Thomas Dixon's book *The Clansman.* "Birth of a Nation" painted a mythological, romanticized version of the original Ku Klux Klan. In the movie, the virtue of Southern Women is rescued by the Klan from leering, sexually animalistic black men (white actors in blackface). The film is saturated with the worst sort of racial stereotyping and bigotry—black legislators take off their shoes and socks and eat fried chicken maniacally in the state legislature, for instance. Many of the iconic images we now associate with the Klan such as white sheets and burning crosses were actually invented for the film.

The film was controversial from the start. In Boston, Philadelphia and other cities, race riots began. One white man in Lafayette, Indiana, killed a black teenager after seeing the movie. The newly formed NAACP condemned the film as "three miles of filth" and helped get "Birth of a Nation" banned completely in cities such as Chicago, Denver, St. Louis, Pittsburgh and Kansas

City. But in the South, where a white population still harbored deep resentment over Reconstruction, the film's imagery caught fire.

Soon a new Klan was on the march. In the late teens, membership skyrocketed toward six million—or one quarter of the eligible male population in the United States. And it was not just blacks that were subjected to the Klan's terror. Catholics, Jews and immigrants were also on the KKK's hit list. And as the group gained in political power and took control of state governments in Tennessee, Indiana and Oklahoma, Klan leaders attempted to spread their message to new parts of the country. In 1923, the KKK headed for Palo Alto.

Initial Klan activity in Palo Alto came from a Texas engineering graduate student at Stanford University named Robert Burnett. A 1923 article appearing in the *Palo Alto Times* reported on Burnett's desire to organize a local chapter of the KKK. By 1924, two groups had been formed—one at Stanford, including at least seven faculty members—and another in Palo Alto, said to represent a wide array of local businessmen. A women's branch comprising more than 50 members was established later that year.

And although it's hard to imagine today, the Klan was not shy about making public appearances in Palo Alto. In August 1924, for instance, robed Klansmen, defiantly perched in the open backseats of fifteen automobiles, were led by the Oakland Klan Band in a march down Alma Street and Hamilton Avenue. The event was witnessed by several hundred Palo Altans.

In March of that year, hooded Klansmen burned fiery crosses and initiated 31 new members in a ceremony near Pitman and Katherine Streets, witnessed by some 500 spectators.

The Klan also seems to have had some political power in town. Police Chief Chester F. Noble accused the Klan of being behind a residential committee's effort to bring him down on charges of corruption. Responding to accusations of pocketing police money for personal use, Noble told reporters, "I know positively that this is merely a Klan fight against me. I have received regular reports of Klan meetings from two Klan members who have kept me personally informed. I know who the members of this organization are and many of them are prominent on this committee."

The Klan was probably retaliating against the chief's recent anti-Klan crackdowns: according to a 1946 *San Francisco Chronicle* article, Noble had called for help from San Francisco police chief Dan O'Brien, who sent in "25 rookie coppers, dressed as civilians and swinging saps…" Noble had also dismissed a number of Klansmen from his own police force.

Rev. Thomas Dixon had no regrets about the resurgence of the Klan brought about by his book and the movie based on it. [WIKIPEDIA COMMONS/L.C. PAGE & COMPANY, 1903]

D.W. Griffith, the legendary director of "The Birth of a Nation." He is said to have regretted the impact of the film and sought to make amends with a later film "Intolerance." [WIKIPEDIA COMMONS/CIRCA 1925]

And it was not only Palo Alto's police who made it clear that they were not welcome in town. In February 1924, the KKK was denied permission by commanding officer Lawrence Cook to use the Naval Reserves Drill Hall for a meeting where official California Klan lecturer James Bronson was set to address the membership. The Klan was then denied the use of De Luxe Hall, as well, after the owner was spooked by a letter from Monsignor Joseph Gleason threatening a Catholic boycott. In the previous year, the Stanford chapter of the Klan was denied use of campus buildings by Stanford University president Dr. Ray Lyman Wilbur, who at the same time, forbade the Klan from associating Stanford's name with a university-based KKK.

Without an indoor venue in which to hold meetings, the Palo Alto Klan was often forced to gather outdoors. In August of 1924, for instance, a group initiation had to be held rather unceremoniously in a vacant lot between Emerson and Alma streets. Although the Klan had gained a toehold in Palo Alto, it did not find the city ripe for exploitation. The Klan would soon move on.

Two decades later, however, the city worried over a second coming of the Klan. Local residents awoke on May 31, 1946, to find a three-foot-high red-lettered KKK insignia painted at the intersection of Homer and Ramona streets, situated in what was then a small black area of town surrounding the A.M.E. Zion Church. Police Chief Howard Zink believed that the work was "done by an organization, not pranksters." The symbol's unfortunate appearance seemed a harbinger of other troubles that swirled in the Midpeninsula during the mid-1940s. The height of area KKK activity came later that year, when the Klan burned down the house of John Walker, a black man who had moved into an all-white Dumbarton Oaks neighborhood of Redwood City.

But condemnation of the Klan in Palo Alto was swift and strong. Local op-eds asked the police to "arrest and prosecute the Klansmen" and urged local citizens "not to rest until we have found the Klan members living here and taken appropriate action." A third *Times* writer warned that "by shutting our eyes to the first ventures of these un-American cowards at whatever level they operate, we leave the way open for activities that undermine our democracy and stain the fine community reputation we are so smug about."

The Ku Klux Klan would never again reach its heady heights of the 1920s—either here in Palo Alto or across the nation. The PC culture of the modern mass media probably helps to keep any resurrections at bay. Television, movies, and the Internet have been great equalizers in dictating what is acceptable in our society—and the Ku Klux Klan is certainly not.

KKK insignia painted on street. May 31, 1946, [REDWOOD CITY TRIBUNE]

Police Chief Chester Noble blamed the Klan for the effort to bring him down. [PALO ALTO TIMES]

Opening ceremony for the new Embarcadero Underpass, 1936.

THE EMBARCADERO UNDERPASS
Accident Before Action

SINCE THE DAYS WHEN THE AUTOMOBILE FIRST GAINED WIDESPREAD POPULARITY, THERE has been an on-going geographical competition between cars and trains. As roads and highways began to crisscross the land, an emerging web of intersecting pavement met an older web of steel and girders that was the national railroad system. And each time they crossed, there was the potential for disaster, as one form of transportation met another.

As a result, eliminating dangerous grade crossings has been on nearly every city and state's to-do list. Over time, overpasses or underpasses were built to separate grades at thousands of intersections across the country, but even today thousands more remain potential danger spots.

Of course, Palo Alto was a train town from the beginning. As the companion settlement to a university founded by a railroad magnate, the city was built around the train depot at the base of University Avenue. Since the onset of the automobile and the construction of its requisite highways and byways, city fathers worried about the intersection of train and car. Originally, these grade crossings consisted primarily of four major intersections—across Palo Alto Avenue near the Menlo Park border, at busy University Avenue, at California Avenue in the southern end of town and at Embarcadero Road.

It was this last juncture that concerned the most citizens. In 1919, what was then known as Palo Alto Union High School was built at the southeast corner of Embarcadero and El Camino Real just across from the train tracks. At the time, this location was a bit out of the way, but it satisfied the political realities of the high school "union" between Palo Alto and Mayfield. Although the two cities would merge entirely in 1925, a central location was of political importance at the time of the school's founding.

An article about the accident which killed Mary C. Harris and Max Springer, 1927. [PALO ALTO TIMES]

Because more than 250 students reached Palo Alto Union High School by crossing the tracks by either car or foot, the location concerned both parents and school officials. Vague promises were made to build an underpass at Embarcadero Road for cars and pedestrians, but the high school opened in 1919 without one, greatly worrying Principal Walter Nichols.

Before the school even opened, Principal Nichols had embarked upon a determined campaign to try to convince city, state or county officials to build an underpass at the intersection. In a letter to Palo Alto's Board of Public Safety in July 1924, Nichols dramatically warned that "It is as certain as the rising sun that a Palo Alto child will be carried home in a hearse from this corner sooner or later." In his lobbying, Nichols was highly critical of the Southern Pacific Railroad. At one point he incredulously quoted a congratulatory letter he had received from S.P. on the high school's "efforts to prevent damage to its engines and trains." He also reported that the railroad had told him that there was no need for an underpass because "thus far there are no fatal accidents that have occurred there."

At 8:45 a.m. on the morning of October 26, 1927, Mary Collins Harris and Max Springer, both 17, were on their way to attend the Palo Alto Junior College located on the high school campus. As they reached the rail crossing, flagman Emmet Bennett waved at Springer's car to stop as the Southern Pacific Shoreline Limited #78 barreled toward the intersection. But for some reason Springer never did stop as his car made the turn toward the high school. As it crossed the tracks, the automobile was struck full-force just behind the rear wheel by the oncoming train, sending the vehicle nearly 50 feet in the air. Both students were thrown out of the car and Mary Harris died instantly. Springer died later at Palo Alto Hospital.

Students at the high school and junior college were devastated. Mary Harris, whom friends called "Polly," was an only child and native of Melbourne, Australia. She had planned to attend Pomona College and was active in the Girl Scouts. Max Springer was the son of prominent Palo Alto Judge John Springer and had been student commissioner of athletics at Palo Alto High School, from which he graduated before continuing on to the Junior College.

On the same day as the horrific crash, bereaved students at the Palo Alto Junior College passed resolutions asking for the immediate construction of an underpass at Embarcadero Road. It read: "Since 1916, the faculty of the high school and the citizens of Palo Alto have consistently urged the construction of a subway. We, being minors who have no vote, can only protest in this

Palo Alto Union High School soon after its opening. Right from the beginning many parents and teachers worried about the grade crossing at Alma and Embarcadero (photo circa 1918).

way and petition those whose power is greater than ours to render impossible a repetition of this morning's tragedy."

But it would be another nine years before the underpass was built. Not that there wasn't an effort following the Harris and Springer deaths to remedy the situation. In May of 1929, city voters went to the polls to vote on a $60,000 bond to construct an underpass. Opposing the subway was the Southern Palo Alto Residents Association who believed the project to be "narrow, unsightly and expensive"—and perhaps a bit too far to the north. On Election Day, despite strong support from the *Palo Alto Times* and the offer of financial assistance in construction from Southern Pacific, the bond measure fell just a few votes short of the necessary two-thirds majority.

Eventually, it would take the federal government, rather than Palo Alto's voters, to find money for the Embarcadero Road underpass. It would be built as part of Franklin Roosevelt's New Deal effort to lower national unemployment through public works projects. Palo Alto would get a small chunk of the federal government's $4 million "Grade Separation Program."

Ten months and $160,000 later, a rather extravagant opening ceremony was held for the unveiling of the underpass. The festivities included a lunch-in at Stanford with appearances by the high school band and local Boy Scout troops. Speeches were given by Harry Hopkins, the chairman of the state highway commission, Palo Alto Mayor C. H. Judson and Edward Neron, Deputy Director of Public Works. The *Palo Alto Times* reported that "the first to traverse the subway were a number of children on bicycles and 'kiddie cars' who did not wait for the strains of the anthem to die away to begin the exciting trip." Addressing the elephant that hovered over the celebration, Stanford controller Almon Roth assured the crowd that "every family can rest assured that their children will be protected at this crossing."

Today Caltrain runs on Southern Pacific's old tracks, Mayfield is but a distant memory to South Palo Altans and the junior college on Paly's campus is long gone. But the Embarcadero underpass still stands as it has since 1936, an ordinary looking piece of urban infrastructure with a sad story to tell.

The Embarcadero Underpass under construction in 1936. [PALO ALTO TIMES]

The Japanese Association of Palo Alto marching during the celebration of the opening of the University Avenue underpass, March 1941.

JAPANESE-AMERICAN INTERNMENT
Palo Alto's Deported Patriots

The order that directed Japanese-Americans to their internment fate. [WIKIPEDIA COMMONS/U.S. NATIONAL ARCHIVES AND RECORDS ADMINISTRATION/WAR RELOCATION AUTHORITY]

CIVIL LIBERTIES OFTEN SUFFER DURING WARTIME, A FACT THAT MAY CONTRADICT THE ideological and moral justifications for the wars being conducted. Early patriots passed the highly repressive Alien and Sedition Acts in 1798 to protect against "alien citizens of enemy powers." Abraham Lincoln, in the midst of saving the Union and ending slavery during the Civil War, suspended the right of habeas corpus. At the beginning of the Cold War, as America began a half-century of struggle to bring down the iron curtain of Stalinist Communism, a red scare at home led to McCarthyism, blacklists and the kind of government authoritarianism that reminded many of the Soviet system itself. And in 2001, as the U.S. responded to 9/11 with a war on terror to defend America's way of life, certain freedoms that defined that way of life were being curtailed by the Patriot Act.

Of course, there is a natural tendency for governments to scale back civil liberties during the tension and hysteria that accompanies war. It was in such an atmosphere following the Japanese bombing of Pearl Harbor in December 1941 that the American government committed its most shameful act of wartime repression—the internment of 120,000 Japanese-Americans. Indeed, while "the Greatest Generation" made our nation proud fighting in the Pacific and on the beaches of France to liberate Europe from one of Earth's all-time dictators, the country's moral righteousness was tainted by its actions at home.

In the months that followed the surprise Japanese bombing of Pearl Harbor, America braced itself for a potential follow-up attack on its own shores. It was in this environment that a range of hostile reactions from suspicion to outright racism were directed towards the Japanese-American community. Some West Coast leaders and media organizations questioned the loyalty of

Japanese-Americans, and these flames were fanned by groups of California farmers who cynically saw a chance to obtain profitable Japanese-American farmland. Under pressure, the government slowly began to move toward a policy of outright internment based on ancestry.

In Palo Alto, the small Japanese-American community of about 200 began to worry about their future. In March 1942, local Japanese-Americans were ordered to register their property at Police headquarters on Bryant Street. In April, an 8 p.m. curfew was imposed exclusively on Japanese-Americans, and by the middle of June not a single Japanese-American was left in Palo Alto.

Immediately following Pearl Harbor, many Palo Alto Japanese-Americans feared the worst and some even pleaded their patriotism. Arthur Okado's family had been in America since 1909. But two days after Pearl Harbor, the President of the Palo Alto Japanese Association released a statement printed in the *Palo Alto Times,* saying "We the members of the Japanese-American community having lived in Palo Alto and Menlo Park throughout 40 years… wish to make our stand clear. Without reservation, we are loyal to this, our country, the United States of America."

Interned Japanese-Americans are ironically taught "Democracy at Work" at Heart Mountain in Wyoming.
[WIKIPEDIA COMMONS/U.S. NATIONAL ARCHIVES AND RECORDS ADMINISTRATION/TOM PARKER, 1943]

The article went on to say that the members of the association had purchased some $2,700 in defense bonds and that seven of their men were serving in the Army—including Paly graduate Fred Yamamoto, who would posthumously win the Silver Star after dying in France.

Still, 10 weeks later, Mr. Okado was arrested by FBI agents, along with three other Palo Altans on suspicion of belonging to an "alien Japanese organization." It wasn't until February 1945 that he would return home to Palo Alto cleared of all suspected wrongdoing.

On May 19, 1942, all Japanese-Americans were ordered to leave Palo Alto and the West Coast by Lieutenant General John L. DeWitt upon the authority of President Franklin Roosevelt's Executive Order 9066. Later, DeWitt defended his decision saying, "A Jap's a Jap. We must worry about the Japanese all the time, until he is wiped off the map."

Palo Alto Japanese-Americans had less than a week to sell their homes, farms and businesses—just a small portion of the $400 million nationwide (in 1942 dollars) that Japanese-Americans would lose because of the internment. On May 26, 144 local Japanese-Americans

Most internees from Palo Alto wound up at Heart Mountain in Wyoming. Here a few walk down F Street with spartan-looking barracks are on either side.
[WIKIPEDIA COMMONS/NATIONAL ARCHIVES AND RECORDS/WAR RELOCATION AUTHORITY/TOM PARKER, 1942]

boarded buses leaving for the former racetrack that had been euphemistically renamed the Santa Anita Reception Center. Each person was only allowed to take as much as he or she could carry. An animal ban meant that most family pets had to be destroyed. Japanese-Americans and their Caucasian friends exchanged candy, oranges and other small mementos, while the Palo Alto Society of Friends and the Gray Ladies of the Red Cross brought refreshments, lunch and milk. Then the buses pulled away and they were all gone.

The Palo Altans spent the next few months at Santa Anita before most were moved on to Heart Mountain Relocation Center near Cody, Wyoming. John Kitasako described the scene as they left for Wyoming: "The farewells at the trains are pathetic. Separated friends and even families will not see each other again for the duration [of the war]."

The internment train rides were often horrific. Palo Altan Cherry Ishimatsu would later describe her ride to an Arkansas internment camp: "It was very frustrating, very difficult and a very traumatic experience. It must have taken nine days. The sanitation of the train that you cannot get off of for nine days is horrendous. It was a nightmare." She added that it was extremely hot, the windows were shut for the entire ride and hardly any light reached the inside of the train.

Spirits improved little when most of the Palo Altans reached their final destination and joined 10,000 other Heart Mountain internees. Kitasako reported back to Palo Alto that "our first impression of this center was disillusioning… We could not help but feel we were cut off from the rest of the world." The grim barracks behind barbed wire were primitive at best. The toilets were not partitioned, the beds were simple cots, and the daily budget for food rations was 45 cents per capita. Even Kitasako, an eternal optimist, lamented that "The psychological effects of our confinement have complicated our mental and spiritual structures. We must bolster our morale, we must shake off the outgrowths of penal complexes." More than any hard times or economic loss, most internees remember that the worst part of their experience was the indignity of being treated as a criminal in their own country.

Despite the shame that the nation must bear for the entire internment episode, there is evidence that Palo Alto's record of tolerance in those years was commendable—at least by the standards of 1942. There are few recorded instances of prejudice from locals, and many Caucasians were later honored by Palo Alto Japanese-Americans for their help—visiting and volunteering to teach in the internment camps, sending books, toys, clothing and later providing legal help.

Internees at Heart Mountain in Wyoming.
[WIKIPEDIA COMMONS/U.S. NATIONAL ARCHIVES AND RECORDS ADMINISTRATION/ HIKARU IWASAKI, 1944]

The press of the day also demonstrated sympathy for Palo Alto's friends and neighbors of Japanese ancestry. Paly's newspaper the *Campanile,* reminded readers in 1942 that "They are Americans too… Give them a farewell that will make them want to stay Americans!" And the *Palo Alto Times* opined in May, "When Japanese and Japanese-Americans leave Palo Alto this week, the loss will be ours as well as theirs… Our hearts go out to them in the sorrow and hardship of the uprooting."

Additionally, in the year following the war, James E. Edmiston of the War Relocation Association stated that "no city has done a more complete job than Palo Alto… in helping Japanese and Japanese-Americans reinstate themselves in the community."

Still, few Palo Altans protested or seriously questioned the orders of their government. The *Times* called the policy the "lesser of two evils," believing that it was "necessary for the safety of us all." It wasn't until 1988 that Japanese-Americans nationwide would receive an official apology from their government. The Civil Liberties Act of 1988 acknowledged "the fundamental injustice of the evacuation, relocation, and internment of United States citizens and permanent resident aliens of Japanese ancestry" and provided redress of $20,000 for each surviving detainee.

For many, the legacy of the internment tragedy is the unwavering humanity of the Japanese-American people, as much as the inhumanity of the government that incarcerated them. A few days before the Palo Alto Japanese-Americans were to be forcibly removed from their homes—on a day when anger and hurt must have been raging inside each of them—they sent this letter to the *Palo Alto Times*:

"To the Palo Alto Community: As we leave we would like to express our heartfelt gratitude to the many American friends of this community for their kindness, understanding and fair-mindedness… Needless to say, we are sorry to leave Palo Alto… Many of us have been born here, most of us have gone through all the schools here and some have gone through the university. However, the sorrow that we feel is alleviated in the knowledge that by evacuating, we are cooperating and aiding in the United States' war effort… As we close, we wish to express the hope that we may soon renew our friendship and become part of this community which we regard as our home. We hope that we have been able to express our gratitude for the friendship given to us by the people of this community."

It seems unlikely that any American could love their country more than this.

The most prominent black neighborhood in Palo Alto centered around Ramona Street near the A.M.E. Zion Church.

HOUSING DISCRIMINATION
A Closed Door in Palo Alto

AFTER SUFFERING THROUGH THE AGGRESSIVE RACISM OF THE JIM CROW SOUTH, MILLIONS of African-Americans left for the industrial cities of the North and the supposedly tolerant climate of California in the three decades following World War II. But if they found there a less confrontational form of racism, the effect would often prove every bit as detrimental as the burning crosses and separate drinking fountains of the South. Perhaps most insidious was the housing discrimination they faced in their new surroundings. The actions taken by white property owners and realtors, with a nod from the Federal Housing Administration, would eventually relegate most African-Americans to living in separate and vastly unequal neighborhoods.

While there have certainly been many instances of racial brotherhood and tolerance in Palo Alto, anyone looking back into the city's history must come to terms with the role that racism and bigotry played in the unfair treatment of African-Americans and other minorities. Here, housing discrimination has led to the creation of "two Americas" right in our midst. While largely poor and minority East Palo Alto suffers from crime, unemployment and a troubled school system, just across the freeway Palo Alto thrives after decades of excluding blacks.

In the early days of the city only a few African-American citizens called Palo Alto home. But as their numbers grew and more Asians moved into town as well, attitudes in Palo Alto grew less tolerant. In 1920, the Palo Alto Chamber of Commerce passed a resolution calling for a "segregated district for the Oriental and colored people of the city." The motion was supported by *Palo Alto Times* publisher George F. Morell, as well as the Native Sons of the Golden West, the American Legion and the Palo Alto Carpenters Union. The *Palo Alto Times* ran editorials in support of the idea. Henry Dodson, the president of the Colored Citizens Club of Palo Alto, responded with

Ramona Street looking toward Homer. Once the heart of the African-American community in Palo Alto, it now includes condominiums, businesses and a preschool.
[PHOTO: MATT BOWLING]

dignity and class, stating publicly that "we believe the best people of this city are in unison with the great majority of the people of this state who dissent from such an undemocratic doctrine." He also chastised those who were pushing segregation, saying "Shame on a race that… holds in its hands the wealth of the continent and yet, not only refuses to lift his less fortunate fellow man… but seeks through humiliating, illegal ordinances and discrimination to sink him to the lowest depths of ignorance and vice."

Eventually the plan died, and although racial zones would be suggested again in the 1940s, such segregation was never legislated in Palo Alto. Still, African-Americans would have to fight less vocal racism in the future. For while few Palo Altans demonstrated outward hatred toward minorities or had an inclination to throw white sheets over their heads, there were not many residents who were ready to live next door to a person of color.

The postwar economic boom would bring an influx of southern blacks to the Bay Area. In Palo Alto, their numbers would rise from 239 in 1940 to 467 seven years later, with most African-Americans crowding into a few scattered neighborhoods in town. The most prominent black neighborhood was on Ramona Street near the spiritual home of the community, the University A.M.E. Zion Church. But there were also concentrations of African-American residents on Fife Street near downtown and south of Colorado Avenue on old El Capitan Road. Conditions on El Capitan Road were described by *Times* Editor Elinor Cogswell in 1951: "These houses stand in tinder dry weeds among mountains of trash… the shacks are not only unsightly but a fire menace. By-passed by the city garbage collectors, the residents [have] to burn such refuse."

As more blacks attempted to move into the city and black residents tried to move out of its ghetto, they met widespread resistance. For instance, the majority of subdivisions established in the city between 1925 and 1950 included the following clause: "No person not wholly of the white Caucasian race shall use or occupy such property unless such person or persons are employed as servants of the occupants…" Other covenants were more informal. When black trucker William Bailey and his family of six moved into the Palo Alto Gardens complex in then mostly white East Palo Alto, residents actually tried raising funds to buy out Bailey to keep it segregated. Hundreds of other such stories never made it to the local press, and most blacks did not even attempt to move across the area's well-known color lines.

The 101 Freeway which divides Palo Alto from East Palo Alto. Originally Bayshore Highway, the 101 now functions essentially as a barrier psychologically if not physically. In the older photo, one can see the former Lucky grocery store at Edgewood Plaza in the far distance at left. [PHOTO ON RIGHT: BRIAN GEORGE]

And some of these lines were essentially sanctioned by the federal government. The Federal Housing Association (FHA) divided properties into four categories for banking purposes, from desirable Type A properties to "risky" Type D properties outlined in red. African-American neighborhoods were almost always put in the D category—a practice later called "redlining." In fact, FHA manuals instructed banks to steer clear of sections with "inharmonious racial groups" and suggested that cities enact racially restrictive zoning ordinances, as well as covenants prohibiting black owners. With such covenants excluding African-Americans from Type A and B neighborhoods and with mortgage loans denied them in Type C and D communities, many blacks faced few options but to rent in urban ghettos. And indeed when an African-American family looked for housing in the Palo Alto area, they usually found the realtor driving into redlined East Palo Alto.

For real estate men, these actions tended to be motivated by profit as much as by bigotry. In 1956 one Burlingame realtor bluntly told the *Palo Alto Times*: "It's pretty well proven that when Negroes come in, property values drop. It's quite a determining factor when I realize I'm going to cost my neighbors two or three thousand dollars." In the same article, Doug Couch, president of Palo Alto's Board of Realtors, agreed, "If you do sell to Negroes, everyone else is down your throat." Couch's estimate of attitudes in Palo Alto was pretty accurate. A 1952 survey by the Palo Alto Fair Play Council reported that only 68 Palo Altans polled would rent to person of good character regardless of race while 198 would rent to Caucasians only.

Some realtors engaged in so-called block-busting schemes, in which agents would stir fears that a neighborhood was about to be inundated by minority residents—and then seek to profit from panic selling. Many parts of East Palo Alto and the Belle Haven district of East Menlo Park experienced this sort of massive "white flight" after a few black residents moved in. Furthermore, when blacks did intentionally break the color line, they often found their white neighbors putting up "For Sale" signs.

Of course, there were groups in Palo Alto that condemned such attitudes and supported open housing. Throughout the 1950s, the Palo Alto Fair Play Committee pushed housing integration by showing documentary films, lobbying government to adopt new laws and helping to improve infrastructure and housing conditions in majority-black neighborhoods. In 1958, over 1,000 Palo Altans signed a petition for "open and unsegregated housing" that was backed by 12 area

Joe Eichler, the famed home builder who insisted that his homes were to be sold to anyone and everyone who had the money.

churches. The petition stated that "all persons are children of God and therefore to be treated as equals under God." And then there was Joe Eichler, the famed Palo Alto home builder who insisted that his homes were to be sold to anyone and everyone who had the money.

All over California, fair housing issues were getting attention. The 1963 Rumford Fair Housing Act to end housing discrimination in California was upended in 1964 when voters passed Proposition 14, an initiative promoted by the California Real Estate Association that essentially banned any government action against housing discrimination. It wasn't until 1967, after the California Supreme Court found that the initiative violated the state constitution, that the U.S. Supreme Court upheld the state decision on the grounds that the realtor's initiative violated the Fourteenth Amendment.

And by the 1970s, although the "black neighborhoods" of Palo Alto were long gone, there were many more advocacy groups fighting for open housing. The NAACP, Midpeninsula Citizens for Fair Housing and the City's own Human Relations Committee had all joined the fight. Still, a 1971 survey by the Midpeninsula Citizens for Fair Housing revealed that racism in housing was widespread. One study showed that 58% of the city's large apartment complexes showed evidence of discrimination when black and white middle class professionals inquired for apartments in sequence.

Two decades later, not enough had changed. The *Palo Alto Weekly* reported that the Midpeninsula Citizens for Housing found racial bias when testing with control subjects. The *Weekly* reported that "blacks who want to live in Palo Alto report they sometimes have trouble finding housing because the apartment or house is 'no longer available'… [but] a white person arriving just a half hour later often finds the apartment available."

Today middle- and upper-class black residents are scattered throughout largely white and Asian neighborhoods in the city. And although recent newspaper reports paint a picture of openness in Palo Alto toward black residents, the legacy of years of housing discrimination is still with us. Despite the massive migration of blacks to the Peninsula in the postwar years, Palo Alto's African-American population still stands at just 2%, as it has since the Great Depression. And if Palo Alto's population does not entirely look like America today, it is clearly because the city shut its doors to some Americans in the past.

Fife Street was once an African-American enclave in Palo Alto. Just two blocks long, the tiny street has changed a great deal in the past five decades.
[PHOTO: MATT BOWLING]

The Oregon Expressway from roughly the same spot more than 40 years apart. [PHOTO ON RIGHT: BRIAN GEORGE, 2012]

THE OREGON EXPRESSWAY
Residentialists Unite

IN POSTWAR AMERICA, THE CAR WAS KING. HAVING LIVED THROUGH TIRE RATIONING, rubber drives and gas restrictions, "The Greatest Generation" had won the war and was ready to hit the road. Reemerging from wartime production plant conversion, the Motor City started working overtime, pushing out the automobiles that would soon become the beloved classics of a golden age of driving. And as Americans set out for the suburbs in the 1950s and began touring Eisenhower's new Interstate Highway System in their '57 Chevys and Ford Thunderbirds, governments were tempted to ram interstate highways through the maze of downtown streets in virtually every American city. City dwellers in tight-knit neighborhoods soon were dwarfed by towering super skyways and divided by six-lane highways barring them from their local grocer or library.

And of course, highway building led to an endless cycle of further automobile dependence. As the new roads were built, more drivers took to their cars—purchasing cheaper homes farther from their jobs, making more shopping excursions to far-away malls and partaking in the new "drive-in culture." As new roads led to new drivers, new drivers led to new traffic. To which city planners often reacted by—you guessed it—building more roads.

It was in this context that Palo Alto fought its own car culture battle in 1961 and '62. While the near-freeway proposed by County planners on the site of old Oregon Avenue was just a mile and a half long—in a small city, this four-lane mega-road was symbolic of Palo Alto's first steps towards bowing down to the dominance of the automobile.

There was certainly a logical basis for the political establishment's desire to widen Oregon Avenue. As one of the crosstown streets that led from the newly upgraded Bayshore Freeway to El Camino Real—and perhaps more importantly—to the Stanford Industrial Park, the two-lane

A cartoonist depicts the fight over Oregon Avenue and the council's various plans to alter it. [PALO ALTO TIMES]

residential street was continuously jammed. By March 1961, public support for a replacement sat comfortably above 70 percent.

But Santa Clara County's original plan for what would replace Oregon Avenue struck many as a gargantuan swath that would split the city in two. Additionally, this plan called for the removal of some 107 homes in order to complete the $2.5 million widening project. The proposal would psychologically separate north and south Palo Alto with four bustling lanes divided by an austere chain fence with just two cross streets—one at Middlefield and one at Louis Road.

A new movement of so-called residentialist opposition began to critique the plan in the local media, and resistance soon reached such a fever pitch that the City Council was moved to reject the plan outright. (The county board was not pleased, later publicly reminding the Council of its "responsibility not only to a few citizens of Palo Alto, but to all the citizens of the county.")

The Council's proposed replacement proved far more appealing. It included a landscaped median strip, six cross streets rather than two, 11 access roads, the removal of the chain link fence, as well as a landscaped south side buffer and landscaped north side service road. Promises were made to keep the speed limit under 30 miles per hour (today the speed limit stands at 35). Such improvements prompted one supporter to say that an "ugly-duckling freeway has changed into a swan of a parkway." Still, even the modified version required the destruction of more than 90 homes and residentialist opposition remained fierce. So, as is typical with controversial matters in California, Palo Alto's City Council stuck it on the June ballot to let the voters decide.

The campaign was heated. A sampling of 1962 op-ed pieces in the *Palo Alto Times* shows how bitter it was. For instance, Patricia Ford of David Avenue expressed the common sentiment that the expressway was just the beginning of the development, "One can only ask whether four or five years from now, when they see their once lovely foothills covered with industry and auto-exhaust haze, can it possibly be that once in a while what is good for Stanford is not necessarily good for Palo Alto." Glenn Wayne of Middlefield Road lobbied against the "slums which are going to develop on both sides of that road" while other residents railed against the forces they saw behind the construction. Councilman Bert Woodward Jr., for instance, told the *Palo Alto Times* that "this whole affair was generated by Stanford University, the Stanford Industrial Park and the downtown merchants. These people still control Palo Alto and I think it's unfortunate." Miriam Patchen of Sierra Court wrote in just "to say 'I told you so' before the rape of Palo Alto."

Sign of the Road: members of the Traffic Action Committee put posters on one of about two dozen cars parked along Oregon Avenue. [PALO ALTO TIMES]

While the strongest words came from expressway opponents, there was ample support in favor of the expressway as well. On November 3, 1961, pro-expressway loyalists staged a public demonstration on Oregon Avenue to show how badly an expressway was needed. Cars were delayed over two hours when "The Traffic Action Committee and Residents of Oregon Avenue Improvement" parked more than 20 cars along the busiest stretch of the road with roof placards with slogans such as "This busy, narrow street is dangerous. Improve Oregon."

The day before the vote the pro-expressway forces were additionally aided by the endorsement of Mayor David Haight, who issued a five-and-a-half page statement correcting "a variety of flagrant distortions of fact" and issuing a last-minute "no trucks on Oregon" pledge. On election day the always fiery Councilman Robert Debs shot back that it was "highly improper" for a councilman to make such a statement at the "last moment with no chance of refutation."

Perhaps it made the difference. The June 5, 1962, voting was extremely tight. While the anti-expressway forces took a 100-vote lead early based on large anti-expressway majorities in South Palo Alto, late evening votes coming in from the Walter Hays area put the expressway over the top. In the end, the road was approved by a razor-thin margin of 9,432 votes in favor to 9,030 opposed. Over the following year, houses were either moved or bulldozed, Oregon Avenue was torn up and the new expressway was constructed.

The official opening of the Oregon Expressway in May of 1964. [PALO ALTO TIMES]

Still, not all was lost for the Residentialists. Despite defeat at the polls, the Oregon Expressway battle turned out to be the initial rallying call for what would eventually become a full-scale Palo Alto political movement. Buoyed by their united opposition, the Residentialists would soon elect council members and take up other fights—eventually bringing down establishment megaprojects such as the Professorville hospital and downtown Superblock project. As Myron Chenard said of the Residentialists shortly after the Oregon vote, "[We] are not folding up… there are going to be other fights and—I predict—other results."

Today a drive down the Oregon Expressway conjures up a mixed legacy. While Palo Alto certainly paid its respects to the dominance of the automobile, its citizens were also early in recognizing the excesses of America's car culture. Unlike many bigger cities in America, local citizens acted in time to save the city from the monolith roadway that might have been. And if Palo Altans must live with four-lane roads crossing their city, well, they could do a lot worse.

The Palo Alto City Council chambers in the old City Hall on Newell Road.

THE 1967 RECALL ELECTION
Palo Alto's Political Rumble

IN THE LATE 1960S, AMERICA SEEMED TO BE COMING APART AT THE SEAMS. A FEELING OF malcontent and revolt seemed to imbibe the nation as authority was challenged everywhere. In hindsight, the 1960s are often remembered as a time when injustices were overcome, when movements succeeded. And certainly it was. But what is sometimes forgotten was how in those years it was not always clear if any progress was being made at all. It sometimes just seemed that the whole country had decided to pick a fight with itself.

And so it was in Palo Alto. 1967 was the year in which long brewing tensions in local politics finally reached a boiling point. The mood inside the City Council chamber mirrored the times, as new progressives challenged the establishment and chaos reigned supreme.

For years, "representative businessmen" had governed Palo Alto without much opposition. But in the 1950s, Palo Alto grew at a dramatic rate, doubling in size from a population of 25,475 in 1950 to 52,287 in 1960. Some worried that growth might continue unabated from the foothills to the bay. Ironically, those who first challenged the city's growth largely came from the newly developed regions. Known as the "Residentialists," they favored slower growth and distrusted large commercial and government projects. In 1962, they found an issue to rally around—opposition to the highly controversial Oregon Expressway. Although the road was eventually built, Palo Alto's first anti-establishment political force solidified in the campaign to oppose it.

Soon the Residentialists began to chip away at the Establishment's power. In 1961, NASA physicist Robert Debs won election as the first Residentialist council member. Two years later he and Enid Pearson led a successful court challenge to the city's practice of spot zoning and forced the adoption of a Master Plan. Residentialists Kirke Comstock and Phillip Flint were elected to

Palo Alto vote at a glance

*denotes winners
(i) denotes incumbent

REGULAR ELECTION
(seats, four-year term)

*Arnold (i)	9,289
Debs (i)	5,292
*Dias (i)	9,109
Gorfinkel	1,420
Marks	4,373
*Spaeth	8,758
Spar	4,607
*Berwald	10,033
Clark	10,946
*Comstock (i)	8,516
*Cooley (i)	9,899
Desposito	5,297
Flint (i)	5,689
Giosso	6,752

RECALL ELECTION
(5 seats, two-year term)

*Beahrs (i)	10,554

RECALL ELECTION
(3 seats, four-year term)

*Gallagher	7,395
Larsen	6,474
*Pearson (i)	7,120
Sher	6,677
*Wheatley	8,240
Worthington (i)	7,036

Charter Amendments

Prop. 1 (recall)	For 4,782	Against 8,441	failed
Prop. 2 (Initiative)	For 3,549	Against 9,905	failed
Prop. 3 (referendum)	For 3,655	Against 9,834	failed
Prop. 4 (candidates' filing)	For 10,830	Against 2,381	passed
Prop. 5 (releasing parkland)	Yes 11,701	No 1,977	passed

The 1967 election's final tally. [PALO ALTO TIMES]

Top to bottom:
Ed Arnold, former Mayor and Establishment Council member.

Frances Dias, Establishment Council member and former Mayor, in 1969, at a Junior Museum ceremony.

Enid Pearson, Council member and Residentialist, in 1969.

the Council in 1963 and then Pearson, Edward Worthington and Byron Sher won in 1965. The council was now divided 7–6, with the Establishment holding a narrow one-seat advantage.

Tension flared. In 1966 gridlock nearly ground the Council to a halt as both sides traded verbal insults and argued over parliamentary procedures. Longtime members Bert Woodward and William Rus regularly referred to the Residentialists as "kooks." Important votes split 7–6 and the Council fell more than a month behind schedule, despite more frequent weekly meetings pushed by Mayor Frances Dias. Walkouts, filibusters, and delaying tactics were commonplace.

In October things got really out of hand when the majority set a meeting for Halloween night. Protesting that this was an evening that should be devoted to family, the Residentialists boycotted the proceedings. But when Residentialist firebrand Robert Debs showed up to officially lodge his protest, things got ugly. A young reporter at the time, Jay Thorwaldson, later *Palo Alto Weekly* editor, described what happened next, "Debs entered the Council chambers through the side door… He said he wasn't staying, as I recall, but had come to object to a Halloween meeting. Councilman Robert "Bob" Cooley… who was about as feisty as Debs… interrupted.

'Shove it, Debs!' he yelled… Debs paused, blinked behind his glasses: 'What did you say?'

'I said, 'Shove it!,'" Cooley repeated slowly.

'Would you like to step outside and say that?' Debs challenged, flushing. Cooley sprang from his chair, circled behind wide-eyed Council members toward Debs. They started back through the side door, opening a door leading to a rear patio.

But City Manager George Morgan, an ex-Marine, raced to interpose himself between the two. Morgan held them apart as they tried to exit—causing them to bump their shoulders on the door frame. Assistant City Manager Cecil Riley pulled Debs away as Morgan held Cooley, and Debs left, shaking his fist."

As the May 1967 election approached, things looked bleak for the Establishment. Because of a previously mandated Council reduction to 11 seats and since more Establishment candidates were up for reelection, the old guard would have to sweep all three seats to hold a one-vote advantage. Given the Residentialist momentum in previous elections, this appeared unlikely.

But a bold plan was concocted by Establishment supporter and local attorney William Love. He formed a 12-member recall committee full of Establishment allies. They would attempt to recall the entire Council—including members of both camps—in hopes of sweeping out most of the Residentialists in one fell swoop. Pressing the case first articulated in the editorial pages of the *Palo Alto Times,* Love argued that the Council's bickering had brought legislating to a standstill. It was time to throw the bums out. By mid-February of 1967, the Recall Committee had managed to collect over 2,000 signatures, enough to put the entire Council up for reelection.

Of course, not all Establishment supporters favored such a strategy. Some Establishment members were outraged at being recalled and three chose not to run again, including Bert Woodward, who said the recall was "a weak and ill-conceived method" of retaliation.

The campaign itself was hectic, as some 21 candidates were running for 11 seats divided into three separate mini-elections: the four-year recall seats, two-year recall seats, and the seats that would have been up for reelection without recall. Perhaps exhibiting more seasoned political acumen, the Establishment candidates worked to exude a moderate image. Positioning themselves in favor of a "balanced community," former mayors Frances Dias and Ed Arnold focused their campaign on maintaining the "residential character of the city." They effectively cast their opponents as rebellious agitators responsible for the infighting on the Council. Meanwhile Frances Dias promised to be a "a vote to unify a fragmented city." While Establishment candidates were certainly slicker, they also benefited from their own political shrewdness.

On the other side, the Residentialist candidates made some political mistakes; they continually lambasted the opposition for the "Great Recall Robbery." Observer and future councilman Joe Simitian believed this was unwise. "Since most voters saw it as a *fait accompli,* the Residentialists reinforced their image of a bickering minority and appeared to be upset over 'sour grapes.'" Outraged by their opponents' political ploy, the Residentialists could never get back on message.

On May 10, the recall effort proved hugely successful. A record turnout expelled four Residentialist incumbents: Robert Debs, Philip Flint, Byron Sher and Edward Worthington. Five novice Establishment candidates won council seats: future mayor Jack Wheatley, Grant Spaeth, John Berwald, Ned Gallagher and the election's top vote-getter, Stanford doctor William Clark. Only the two more conciliatory Residentialists: Kirke Comstock and Enid Pearson were able to hold onto their seats, leaving the Establishment with a 7-2 advantage for the coming session. In the coming decades, the Residentialist movement would take control of city politics for good, winning the battle against entrenched power. But in 1967—as all hell broke loose in Palo Alto politics—it would be the Establishment that would deliver a knock-out blow.

On the cover of the Venceremos newspaper: Sue Flores, Eleanor Kaplan, Gerry Foote and Mort Newman of Chester Street give the salute of solidarity. [PAMOJA VENCEREMOS]

VENCEREMOS
Arming for a Fight

THE LATE 1960S AND EARLY 1970S WERE A TIME OF AWKWARD CULTURAL JUXTAPOSITION, both in the nation at large and here in Palo Alto. Today, pop culture sometimes simplifies those years as a time when the whole society turned into LSD-dropping, free-love-making hippies. But in reality, while the counterculture certainly had a large influence on mainstream life, most Americans were still living according to the rules of the "silent majority."

In a small university town like Palo Alto, the juxtaposition could be even stranger. While hometown locals might be marching in the May Fete Parade on Saturday morning, campus radicals would be clashing with police on Saturday night—all on the same street. It was a time when two countries existed side-by-side, sometimes engaging in a cultural civil war, sometimes pretending the other didn't exist.

One example of this odd Palo Alto political juxtaposition was Venceremos, the Communist radical group headquartered in and around Palo Alto in those years. Founded in 1966 by Aaron Manganiello, the originally Latino left-wing protest organization was named for Che Guevera's battle cry, "We will prevail!" By 1970, Venceremos had evolved into a multicultural Maoist/Communist revolutionary brigade that was a mainstay at any mid-Peninsula protest in those years. Under the leadership of Stanford Professor and Melville scholar H. Bruce Franklin (fired in 1972 for leading a student takeover of the university's computer lab), Venceremos took an active role in community issues and demonstrations.

And these guys weren't fooling around. Venceremos believed that "an unarmed people are subject to slavery at any time." They had secret stashes of rifles, grenades, pipe bombs, and other explosives and they urged members to stay armed at all times—advice that was apparently

H. Bruce Franklin. After being fired by Stanford, he eventually became a professor at Rutgers University.

A banner ad for a People's Rally [PAMOJA VENCEREMOS CIRCA 1971]

followed. With their rifle logo and violent rhetoric, Venceremos startled the local population and caught the eye of federal law enforcement. Many believed they were one of the largest revolutionary groups in the country and a 1972 House Internal Security Committee Report called the group "a potential threat to the United States."

Venceremos' ultimate goal was the overthrow of the government. On their way to armed insurrection, their platform called for (among many other things): "The firing of… profit-motivated murderers, like David Packard and Richard Nixon," "an end to the Fascist court system and fascist judges," and "an education which exposes the lies and oppression created by the corrupt court system and teaches us the true history of oppressed people." Venceremos, enemies of the police, were convinced that "the best pigs are always dead pigs." Pretty radical stuff.

But Venceremos stressed actions over rhetoric. In 1970, they opened a revolutionary community college in a Redwood City storefront that lasted until it ran out of money two years later. They were actively involved in an anti-drug campaign on the streets of Palo Alto in the summer of '71 and later with the Palo Alto Drug Collective. They often showed up at City Council and School Board meetings with a verbal aggressiveness never before seen in Palo Alto's politics. At an August 1971 meeting, for instance, Jeffrey Youdelman shouted down School Board members as "racist, fascist pigs." They also tried to win elections. In May of '71, Venceremos ran Jean Hobson for City Council; she only garnered 798 votes, some 7,000 short of victory. Undaunted, Youdelman ran as a candidate in 1973, but he fared no better. Venceremos member Doug Garrett also ran for Palo Alto School Board and Joan Dolly ran in the 1972 Menlo Park City Council elections.

Venceremos was also part of the ever-present street protest scene that marked Palo Alto counterculture life in the late 1960s and early '70s. Every Saturday night at 7:00 PM, Venceremos held a rally with speakers and bands at Lytton Plaza, which was dubbed "The People's Plaza." This often led to clashes with police as the hour grew late and the music got louder.

The beginning of the end for Venceremos came in 1972, when a number of its members were involved in a headline-grabbing murder. The incident centered around a Venceremos recruit and prison inmate named Ronald Beaty. A habitual stick-up artist and con, Beaty was serving time for armed robbery and kidnapping at Chino Prison. He apparently had romantic ties to Jean Hobson—the former Venceremos candidate for Palo Alto City Council—that would lead to an attempt by the organization to help him escape.

On October 6, 1972, two unarmed prison guards taking Beaty to a court appearance in San Bernardino were ambushed. According to police and Beaty, who became the prosecution's star witness, the government car was forced off a remote highway road near Chino. Four Venceremos members jumped out of two vehicles to set Beaty free. As they prepared to flee the scene, Venceremos member Robert Seabok, 23, shot both guards at point blank range, killing Jesus Sanchez, 24, and wounding his partner George Fitzgerald. Venceremos members Hobson, Seabok, Andrea Holman Burt and Benton Burt were named as the other ambushers. Both Hobson and Seabok were Palo Altans and neighbors, residing on Channing Street not far from downtown.

Hobson and Beaty, possessing a trunkload of weapons, were arrested two months later on the Bay Bridge by San Francisco police. Now wanted for murder on top of past convictions, prosecutors convinced Beaty to sing. He named the four who helped him escape, fingered Robert Seabok as the gunman, and described how others hid him in a rural San Mateo County mountain cabin. Beaty pleaded guilty for his involvement in Sanchez' death and received a life sentence.

In the subsequent trials of 1973 and 1974, Jean Hobson, 19-year-old Andrea Holman Burt and 31-year-old Douglas Burt were all found guilty of second degree murder, while Seabok got life imprisonment and a first-degree murder conviction.

Following legal difficulties related to the incident at Chino, Venceremos began to come apart at the seams. Arguments erupted between various factions in the organization and members began to pull out and join other groups. Venceremos founder Aaron Manganiello also blamed a dope addict in the group's central committee for stealing thousands of dollars from the treasury. By September of 1973, Venceremos had officially disbanded.

Many ex-Venceremos members went on to other organizations, including the Symbionese Liberation Army group that assassinated Oakland superintendent Dr. Marcus Foster at a School Board meeting in November 1973 and then kidnapped newspaper heiress Patricia Hearst in February of 1974. While the SLA never operated in Palo Alto, law enforcement saw substantial links between the two groups.

Today Venceremos has either been forgotten by Palo Altans or is remembered as part of the city's wacky early '70s counterculture. But at their height in 1971 and '72, when they were leading weekly rallies, advocating violent action and shouting down School Board members, Venceremos had more than a few Palo Altans spooked.

The caption to this photo reads, "Mort vs. the Pigs—Tuesday Night." [PAMOJA VENCEREMOS]

Ronald Beaty, escaped Chino detainee, in custody. [PALO ALTO TIMES]

A 1941 photo of the newly built Sea Scout Building designed by Birge Clark.

CLOSING THE YACHT HARBOR
The Battle by the Bay

There have been numerous controversial political battles in the history of Palo Alto, but perhaps none has resulted in as much bitter feeling and long-lasting resentment as the 1980 decision to close the Palo Alto Yacht Harbor. In some ways, it was a classic culture clash. It featured two groups, the yachters and the environmentalists, each possessing vastly different worldviews, with little in common in how they saw the destiny of Palo Alto Harbor. What resulted was perhaps the most compelling political campaign in the city's history. Not only was it exciting, always in doubt and full of rhetorical sparks, but in the end, the campaign itself really mattered. Despite the close divide in public opinion, the environmentalists' campaign was so utterly victorious and the boaters' campaign so profoundly defeated that, by 1985, the public had twice backed what was once almost unthinkable—the complete demolition of the Palo Alto Yacht Harbor.

Before 1980, it seemed rather hard to imagine that the city would ever really close it down. Would the City Council really be responsible for tearing out the docks, piers and yacht buildings, kicking out the well-to-do boaters and letting a functioning harbor return to the mud and weeds of nature? But today a newcomer visiting the former yacht harbor would be hard-pressed to guess that water ever lapped up against the Palo Alto shoreline at all.

In the 1800s, the harbor area served as a major point to transfer goods and people to and from San Francisco and by 1928 the Palo Alto Yacht Harbor had been developed to accommodate local boaters. Over the years, however, the harbor began to change.

How and why it changed was actually a matter of public debate. Boaters said it was because the city allowed airport and golf course developers to divert San Francisquito Creek

A Sea Scout campaigns on Middlefield Road to save the harbor in 1985.

161

The Palo Alto Yacht Harbor in 1985 before the boats were made to leave. This shot looks south toward the hills with the Waste Treatment Plant in the rear.

An aerial view of the Yacht Harbor from 1943 with the Duck Pond in the lower center and Sea Scout building across from it.

and Mayfield and Charleston sloughs, thereby eliminating the natural flushing action of the harbor. The city cited the destruction of local wetlands. Whatever the reason, by the 1950s, the harbor was perpetually filling with silt and bogging down in mud, so that every few years it had to be dredged. This process required excavating an enormous amount of mud (some 50,000 cubic yards) and dumping it on nearby marshlands. Environmentalists contended that this practice was an ecological abomination that over the years had destroyed some 500 acres of tidal marsh. And although Santa Clara County took over the role of the actual dredging of the harbor after Palo Alto's own machinery broke in 1957, the city still had to pay for the cost of moving the mud.

Some of the members of the more environmentally friendly Council elected in 1978 were opposed to such a questionable and expensive policy for so many to support the boating of so few. And so on June 2, 1980, they surprised many observers by agreeing to dredge the harbor only one more time in 1981 and then to allow it to dry up and return to its "natural state."

Yacht owners hit the roof. Not only were there more than 120 boats docked at the harbor and few other available berths in Northern California, but the Palo Alto Yacht Club had become a way of life for a small group of marine enthusiasts. The harbor was also the home to the highly popular Sea Scouts. The boaters quickly got organized, collected nearly 5,000 signatures and managed to put the issue on the November 1980 ballot. It would be the city's voters who would decide the fate of the Yacht Harbor.

The pro-harbor forces had also brainstormed an alternative to dumping in marshland. As it so happened, at the time, the city was looking for a way to turn its ever-growing dump into landfill, as had been recently been mandated by the state. So the yachters proposed turning lemons into lemonade by using the dried mud dredged from the harbor to cover the garbage. It would be the cost of this proposal that became a key topic of debate during the campaign.

As both sides attempted to woo voters in the fall of 1980, statistics became a source of contention. For instance, harbor opponents such as City Council member Emily Renzel said using topsoil from a nearby abandoned International Telephone & Telegraph plant would be a million dollars cheaper than using dredged mud from the harbor to cover the dump. Boaters vehemently disagreed, saying that their plan was actually the more economical. Furthermore, the pro-yacht forces argued that the harbor would only need to be dredged once every three years, while their opponents said that the correct figure was actually closer to three times each year.

The statistical disagreements contributed to a tense debate on October 9, 1980, between harbor supporter Dan Peck and Mayor Alan Henderson. As reported in the *Peninsula Times Tribune,* Peck first accused Henderson of knowingly sabotaging a plan to dredge the harbor in order to doom the boaters. Then Peck said that the mayor was "perpetuating a lie" in promoting the three-times-a-year statistic. Henderson, visibly irritated, shot back that "he hoped personal attacks would be avoided." As Election Day approached, both groups repeatedly traded barbs in the local press. Meanwhile, voters were left rather bewildered. With so many numbers and plans flying about, the average voter had little idea whose statistics were correct.

But it was here that the more politically savvy anti-harbor campaign stepped into the void. With financial estimates in such dispute, they presented a more emotional, visceral argument that seemed to convince many Palo Altans that the harbor was not worth saving. They were able to effectively use campaign literature and print advertising to paint the boaters as elitist and exclusionary—ultra-rich executives abusing the public coffers by making the city pay to dredge their water playground. One anti-harbor ad showed an ominous black and white photo of the "members only" sign at the Palo Alto Yacht Club. And campaign literature rhetorically asked voters if they were willing "to pay more than a $1,000 per boat subsidy per year to 108 boat owners (only 40 of whom live in Palo Alto)?" And it seemed that no matter how many times the boaters professed to being just "middle-income people," they could not convince the public. The accusation had stuck.

On November 4, 1980, Palo Altans voted down a measure by a 54–46% margin that would have continued dredging and saved the harbor. At the time it seemed likely Palo Alto had seen the end of the yacht harbor debate.

And yet, five years later the yachts were still there. In the meantime, the Palo Alto Harbor Association had been able to keep the harbor operational by acquiring its own dredge and leasing the docks and piers from Santa Clara County. And as the decreed 1986 closing date for the harbor approached, the boaters managed to put the issue back on the election ballot. This time the voters were asked to allow the harbor to stay open if yachters did their own dredging. But by 1985, the environmental movement had further matured in Palo Alto and harbor opponents successfully argued that the dredging and mud-dumping required was too harmful to local marshlands. The public voted to close the harbor again—this time by a 55–45% margin.

Emily Renzel was an adamant opponent of the Yacht Harbor during her time on the Palo Alto City Council; photo circa 1980s.

The former Sea Scout Building in 2012 as it looks out on the former bay. [PHOTO: BRIAN GEORGE]

After the 1985 election, the yachters' actions became increasingly desperate. After obtaining the legal representation of former U.S. Representative Pete McCloskey, they sued the city, arguing that the closing of the harbor violated the California Constitutional guarantees that ensure public access to navigable waterways. A Santa Clara County Superior Court judge dismissed the suit. And even by 1987, after the city had dismantled virtually all traces of the harbor and all but a few abandoned boats had fled, the Palo Alto Harbor Association was still trying to raise $20,000 to take its case to the California Supreme Court. Even in the late 1990s, there were angry old harborites like perpetual City Council candidate Edmund Power, who raged against the council for their "immorality" in closing the harbor.

Today, looking across the mud toward the lonely posts standing in weeds alongside the decaying Sea Scout building, one wonders if the vitriol of that campaign didn't hurt Palo Alto in the end. While a forward-thinking Council certainly took bold actions to help the environment, at times they seemed more interested in beating their opponents than working towards a compromise. Somewhere in the fierceness of the debate of 1980, the yacht harbor issue seemed to become a zero sum game. And when yachters lost in the end, the city seemed to lose something as well.

CITIZENS

This two room schoolhouse on Bryant Street between University and Hamilton Avenues was built in four days by the "able-bodied men" of Palo Alto.

ANNA ZSCHOKKE
The Mother of Palo Alto's Schools

PALO ALTANS HAVE ALWAYS TAKEN GREAT PRIDE IN THEIR COMMUNITY. SURE, EVERY TOWN has its boosters, but Palo Alto residents seem to feel a true interrelationship with their neighbors and the city as a whole. Watchful parents keep a close eye on the public school system, preservationists keep a close eye on city landmarks, and these days, online bloggers seem to keep a close eye on just about everything else. These folks really care.

The tradition of caring in the community goes back to Palo Alto's earliest residents—in fact, its very first. (And yes, there actually was a first resident.) She was Anna Zschokke, a widowed German immigrant and mother of three who first settled in a house along Homer Street. Zschokke became the city's first historian, was known as a prominent socialite and was eventually dubbed the "Mother of the Palo Alto Schools." And it turns out she was not only Palo Alto's first resident, but one of its most generous.

In 1896, one of Palo Alto's early weeklies, the *Palo Alto Live Oak,* published a "Pioneer History of the Town of Palo Alto" as authored by Mrs. Anna Zschokke. It would prove to be a remarkable article. Reprinted in the *Palo Alto Times* again in 1917, Zschokke's account was a record of enormous detail about the town's formative years. It gave a chronological account of the earliest residents' arrivals, births and deaths, as well as construction projects, street gradings, housing starts and on and on. Her memories painted the scene of that still-unsettled Palo Alto—when just four houses lay scattered along Embarcadero Road, an open shed constituted Palo Alto's main train depot, and a horse-and-buggy taxi coming from Menlo Park could wander for hours just trying to locate some place known as "Palo Alto."

Anna Zschokke with sons Arthur and Theodore and daughter Irma. [FREMONT ZSCHOKKE]

Zschokke had actually lived quite an eventful life before ever setting foot in Palo Alto. Born in Germany in 1849, she moved to America at the age of three, later living in Indiana, and in Kern and Santa Clara counties in California. But after the death of her husband Oscar, she took her three children on the road again—this time north to the new town being laid out in the shadow of the nearly completed Stanford University. Along with six other families, the Zschokkes spent many weeks camped under the trees while their houses were being constructed. It would be the Zschokke residence on Homer Avenue that would be ready first. When the family trouped over the threshold, Anna Zschokke became Palo Alto's first resident. Still, these were lonely days as the first families waited for a town to sprout up around them. Anna recalled that in those early months, "we overcame the loneliness of our situation by entertaining each other with tea parties and making a celebration of every child's birthday. Christmas Day brought us together at one home, New Year's at another and Washington's Birthday at still another." Palo Alto enjoyed the utmost in community bonds in that first year.

The Zschokke-financed house which served as Palo Alto's first high school until 1901. After the high school moved to its new location on Channing Avenue, the Zschokkes used the house as a residence.

Zschokke took to recording the town's early history with the fervent belief that it would someday be an important place. Zschokke noted all firsts: the first-born baby (Andrew McLachlan, Jr.), the first wedding (Mrs. N. Mosher and Mr. N. W. Harper), the first Sunday services ("held under the trees near the lumber yard for we needed its planks for seats"), and even the first accident, when "On August 30th, 1890, we had the terrible experience of Mr. L. Gillan's sudden death, caused by the Sunday Monterey Express running over him."

Also recorded were the deeds of J. Hutchinson's Palo Alto Improvement Club which was working hard to bring essentials to a town that was growing rapidly—from a population of just 37 souls at the start of 1891 to 73 on New Year's Eve, to 300 residents by the end of 1892, and thanks to a great emigration from Mayfield, to 750 by the close of 1893. A supply of water, grading of the major streets, sewerage, electric light, street railways, and water works were all on the early agenda for city improvements. Zschokke also took note of businesses first appearing in Palo Alto. Just a sample—the first book store opened by H. W. Simkins in the old Wigle building on High Street and E. F. Weishaar ran the first grocery store located (rather oddly) in the north room of the Palo Alto Hotel. And Zschokke recalled the boost in city pride when the first issue of the long-running *Palo Alto Times* debuted on January 3, 1893. All in all, the Zschokke history provides an interesting glimpse at how a town first came to be.

But Zschokke wasn't just a passive observer. She displayed a passionate drive for civic improvements—especially when concerned with the betterment of children. And the degree to which she was willing to help her young town would prove remarkable. As an increasing number of small children moved in, Zschokke reported that "Mothers sighed over the drawback of having to send the little ones so far as Mayfield (two miles)." And while Zschokke and her supporters were able to convince the County Superintendent that building Palo Alto's first public school would be a good idea, Mayfield disagreed, claiming that their upstart neighbors to the north were still within their two-mile jurisdiction.

By 1893, after measurements proved that was not quite so, Palo Altans footed the bill for a temporary schoolhouse. In a true show of community spirit, "all able-bodied men" were summoned to come help erect the new two-room schoolhouse. In four days it was up and ready for reading and writing.

After a larger school was built at Webster and Channing in 1894, Zschokke became interested in the need for a school for older boys and girls. For a time, a high school opened in the cramped top quarters of the elementary school, but Zschokke knew this solution was only temporary. So she mortgaged her house, bought a lot herself, hired a contractor and built a three-room schoolhouse with good plumbing—with help from a family trust in Switzerland. Taking bits of cardboard cut to scale to represent furniture, Zschokke then worked out how to make the small structure serve as a working, if only temporary, high school.

Her friends thought she had gone off the edge. They tried to convince her that the plan was financially doomed, that high school students would damage her property and that she was mortgaging away her future. But build it she did. And when she ran out of space as enrollment grew, Zschokke built another shack behind the house to serve as a science lab.

That little house served four years as the high school while the city procrastinated about building a real high school on Channing. When they did, she was able to turn the old classrooms into her new living room and bedrooms.

For her extreme generosity in the early years of the city's education, Anna Zschokke has often been called the "Mother of the Palo Alto schools." From those early days of shacks and bungalows, Palo Alto's schools would grow to be admired across the state. But it all began with Resident Number One.

Channing Avenue, the center of education in Palo Alto in the 19th century. The elementary school is on the left and the high school on the right. [THE CAROLYN PIERCE POSTCARD COLLECTION]

Birge Clark in 1975. [PHOTO: CAROLYN CADDES]

BIRGE CLARK
An Architectural Legacy

IT'S RARE THESE DAYS THAT A SINGLE ARCHITECT CAN HAVE A GREAT INFLUENCE ON THE look of a single city. But in days past before the big architectural firms, occasionally local architects could essentially design their own cities, integrating entire blocks of buildings and giving a city a comprehensive theme. Birge Clark did not lay out Palo Alto in the way that urban grids were surveyed in Washington D. C. by Peter Charles L'Enfant or in Philadelphia by Thomas Holme. But he had a major influence over the look of Palo Alto by building many of its most important civic structures and houses—much as Brasilia's Oscar Niemeyer or San Diego's Irving Gill did for larger metropolises. During a career spanning five decades, Clark designed 98 Palo Alto houses and nearly 400 buildings in and around town—including the downtown Post Office, two major hotels, the Community Center, police and fire building, Children's Library, the Sea Scout Building and on and on. In many ways, Palo Alto today is a realization of the architectural imagination of Birge Clark.

Birge Clark's father was an architect, Stanford professor and mayor of Mayfield. A longtime friend of Herbert Hoover, Arthur Clark constructed the future president's home in 1919 with assistance from young Birge. After attending Palo Alto High, Stanford and Columbia University, Birge served in World War I, earning the Silver Star for Gallantry after being shot out of an observation balloon by a German pilot and parachuting to safety. Returning home to Palo Alto, he set up shop in 1922, becoming one of just two licensed architects working between San Jose and San Francisco. Like a country doctor, Clark did a little of everything—houses, schools, public buildings, libraries. And as the city grew in the first half of the twentieth century, Clark was the only architect in town.

Birge and Lucile Clark at the Lucie Stern Community Center, circa 1976. [PHOTO: CAROLYN CADDES]

The Clark-designed Hotel President which was named for Stanford's Herbert Hoover, a friend of Birge. [THE CAROLYN PIERCE POSTCARD COLLECTION.]

He was also immensely talented. In his early days, Clark worked almost exclusively in the fairly short-lived, but locally popular architectural style, variously referred to as Spanish Colonial Revival, California Colonial or the closely related Mission Revival. Although there were variations, the style most often consisted of stucco wall, red clay roof tiles, cast concrete ornaments and wrought-iron grilles. Popular between 1915 and 1931, this romantic fashion caught on in many places with a Spanish past: Florida, Texas and especially California.

In Santa Barbara, the style became so popular that the city government actually legislated all buildings to be constructed in Mission Revival style—with compulsory specifics written into law. In Palo Alto, the style dominated more naturally, in part because it recalled a Spanish past that was at the root of El Palo Alto and the city's founding.

But while Spanish motifs may have been all the rage in 1920s California, things were a little different back East. Presenting his blueprints for Palo Alto's post office to the nation's postmaster general in Washington, Clark was ridiculed. As long-time employee and associate Joseph Ehrlich tells the story, "The postmaster pushed them away and said, 'Don't you know what a U.S. post office looks like? We expect a stately building with neo-Romanesque columns showing the power of the federal government. I cannot approve this design.'…Birge responded, 'Ok, but I don't think the President and First Lady are going to be pleased with the design change.'" After revealing that the Hoovers had already approved the plans while Clark was breakfasting with his old friends that morning, the postmaster had a sudden change of heart and signed off on every blueprint in front of him.

During his life, Clark always admitted to being lucky. During the Great Depression when many architects closed up shop, Clark stayed in business in large part doing work for Kaiser Permanente and Palo Alto's prime benefactor, Lucie Stern. Thanks to Stern's generosity, Clark built some of his most memorable structures such as the recently renovated Children's Library and the Lucie Stern Community Center.

And although Clark became most famous for his Spanish-influenced works like the Roth Building on Homer Avenue, the Hotel President on University Avenue and the Medico-Dental Building on Hamilton Avenue, he also ventured into other styles during the later part of his career. His "Streamline Moderne" buildings include the former Pontiac dealership at 790 High Street and the recently renovated Sea Scout building (designed to resemble a ship) out in the

Baylands. He also played with the "form equals function" credo of modernism, especially in his work for Hewlett-Packard and Stanford.

Finally, many of the city's best known and most prestigious homes were also built by Clark, including the Norris House at 1247 Cowper Street, the Dunker House at 420 Maple Street and Lucie Stern's own house at 1990 Cowper. And one street still stands as a kind of Birge Clark museum, as he designed every one of the homes on Coleridge Avenue between Cowper and Webster streets.

Palo Alto has been called "The City that Birge Built" and the work of his career remains on display all over town. Before his death in 1989, Clark told an interviewer, "You know they say a doctor buries his mistakes, and a lawyer's mistakes go to prison. All an architect has to do to see his mistakes is drive around the block." Take a drive around Palo Alto's blocks these days and one thing you won't find are many Birge Clark mistakes.

Top, the Kathleen Norris house.

Left, the downtown post office soon after completion.

"The portrait of the late President John F. Kennedy was draped with black crepe in the empty Palo Alto post office today..." read the headline and photo caption on November 23, 1963.
[PALO ALTO TIMES]

JFK AT STANFORD
Days of Decision

THE ASSASSINATION OF JOHN F. KENNEDY BROUGHT THE NATION TOGETHER IN A PROfound way. In those still relatively early days of mass media, the country experienced its first significant television moment on that November Friday in 1963. Millions of Americans sat in their living rooms looking at television boxes as Walter Cronkite tried to keep his composure announcing, "From Dallas, Texas, the flash—apparently official—President Kennedy died… some 38 minutes ago." The country would unite in a way not experienced in years.

Of course, it wasn't just the shooting of the president and the confirmation of his death that mesmerized the nation, but the entire insane course of events that weekend. The arresting of Oswald, his bizarre and chaotic murder on live television, the apprehension of Jack Ruby, LBJ's airplane oath next to Jackie in the blood-soaked dress, and on and on.

Like the rest of the country, Palo Altans were jarred by the news. When an announcement was made to students at Palo Alto High School, the *Palo Alto Times* reported that "the assembly became a scene of anguish and hysteria. Some students wept openly, some cried out and others got up and raced out of the hall." As events unfolded, much of the city was glued to their televisions that surreal weekend. The day after the shooting, the *Times* said that "the streets, the playgrounds, the stores, the schools—all were empty." In the downtown post office on Hamilton Avenue hung a black-draped painting of the slain president, while his portrait was displayed in many storefront windows. Nearly everything in town was cancelled that weekend. The Big Game itself was postponed by a week for the only time in the long history of the contest.

On Sunday morning, special services were held at the Foothill College gymnasium and Stanford Memorial Church as well as at St. Thomas Aquinas Church, St. Ann's Chapel and St. Mark's.

JFK in his presidential years. [WIKIPEDIA COMMONS/ U.S. LIBRARY OF CONGRESS, 1961]

Nearly everything in town was canceled or closed: Stanford Shopping Center parking lot (above) and downtown Menlo Park (below).

Editorials in local papers also mourned President Kennedy. The *Palo Alto Times* stated that "Today a shocked America feels an aching void" and that "We shall deeply miss a courageous young captain." Readers who wrote in to honor the fallen president were already trying to figure out who was behind the murder. A debate had begun that lives on to this day.

Although certainly not all Palo Altans knew it at the time, the city had briefly played host to John F. Kennedy some 23 years earlier. During the fall of 1940, a young JFK had spent a few pivotal months at Stanford University as he audited business school classes and tried to figure out what to do with his life. It was a turning point for the recent Harvard graduate who at the time was being pulled in a great many directions.

Although he was the son of Joseph Kennedy, the wealthy businessman and Ambassador to the United Kingdom, young Jack was not necessarily the chosen son. That role had been reserved for his older brother Joe Jr., who was already at Harvard Law and seemed destined for great things. Not that the second Kennedy boy was any sort of black sheep. With some help from his father, he had already become a best-selling author after publishing his senior thesis on English appeasement as the book, *Why England Slept*. The Harvard yearbook had even named Jack Kennedy "Most likely to become president."

But Kennedy was perhaps not as confident about his future as were his peers. For one, he was constantly battling health problems. Along with jaundice and digestive troubles, JFK had recently injured his back playing tennis and spent 10 days in bed at the Lahey Clinic. And Kennedy seemed a bit unsure about a career path. He had thoughts of becoming "an author or writer of some sort," possibly following his father into business or maybe going to law school. Besides, as war loomed on the horizon, nobody Jack's age really knew what the future held.

So having heard his Harvard roommate Tom Killefer extol the beauty and climate of Stanford University, Jack figured he'd head out to California, get some warmth for his ailing back and audit a few classes at the Stanford Business School while waiting to see what happened next.

In mid-September 1940, Kennedy arrived in Palo Alto in his brand-new cactus green Buick convertible with red seats and checked into the President Hotel on University Avenue. After getting a lay of the land, he rented the one-bedroom cottage behind the campus house of Miss Gertrude Gardiner at 624 Mayfield Avenue. For $60 a month, it was a pretty good deal, plus he didn't have to pay for a new bed as he slept on a plywood board at night to help his back.

As it turned out, Kennedy wasn't really all that interested in business studies. Politics was his field of choice, as evidenced by his participation in Professor Thomas Barclay's seminar analyzing the on-going 1940 presidential race as well as taking "Contemporary World Politics" with Professor Graham Stuart. Jack had thoughts of his own on the war and they bent toward a more hawkish stance than those of his father.

But despite his clear intelligence and interest in academics, Jack was also living the fast life for which the Kennedy men would become rather famous. Jack was well-known on El Camino's restaurant row, entertaining the ladies at L'Omelette and Dinah's Shack regularly. He dated lots of San Francisco girls, driving up and back to the city at dangerous speeds on Bayshore Highway. He also spent some time downstate with the Hollywood set, palling around with family friends like Robert Stack and meeting the likes of Clark Gable, Lana Turner and Spencer Tracy—and lots more girls.

During his stay at Stanford, the prospect of potential American involvement in the war continued to grow. In mid-October of 1940, the peacetime draft was enacted, a measure supported by Kennedy, who was a member of the Stanford National Emergency Committee. Kennedy registered on campus on October 18, with some apprehension—not because he worried about serving, but because he feared he could not. Due to his bad back and other ailments, it seemed unlikely that Jack would ever put on a uniform. But as he wrote to friend Lem Billings, "They will never take me in the Army and yet if I don't go, it will look quite bad." A year later, family connections would help him become a Navy lieutenant, where he won the Navy and Marine Corps Medal as commander of the famed boat, PT-109.

John Kennedy's stay at Stanford would come to a rather anti-climactic end. A trip back east to help his father write his memoirs took him away from campus. Kennedy planned to return to Stanford for the spring term, but his passion and heart lay not at Stanford and the business school but in politics and World War II. Instead of returning to Stanford in 1941 he ended up travelling to South America and then making his way into the United States Navy.

Years later as those in Palo Alto mourned the passing of the president, there were many at Stanford for whom the tragedy hit especially hard. For they knew Jack Kennedy.

Above: A young JFK in Navy uniform, c. 1942. Below: JFK on board PT-109, c. 1943. He would win a medal for his heroics. [WIKIPEDIA COMMONS/JFK PRESIDENTIAL LIBRARY AND MUSEUM, BOSTON]

William Shockley at home in the garden. [PHOTO: CAROLYN CADDES, PORTRAITS OF SUCCESS, 1985]

WILLIAM SHOCKLEY
"Paranoia Strikes Deep..."

IT IS UNLIKELY THAT ANY PALO ALTAN HAS EVER LIVED A LIFE AS IMPORTANT AS WILLIAM Shockley. As a young man during World War II, he won the nation's highest civilian honor for discoveries that saved thousands of lives. In 1956, he won the Nobel Prize in Physics for the invention of the transistor, a device that either made possible or greatly improved nearly every modern gadget we use today. He then moved west and started the company that became the catalyst for the rise of Silicon Valley. He was even named one of the 100 most important people of the 20th century by *Time Magazine* in 1999. And yet despite this resumé of accomplishment and his indisputable intelligence, William Shockley always seemed to find a way to allow his personality to spoil his own success.

William Shockley seemed to enter the world in the midst of a fight. Born in London in 1910 to American parents, Shockley's early childhood was something between tempestuous and the taming of a beast. When William was just a month old, his father wrote in his diary that his child "gives signs of having a violent temper." Indeed, he was soon biting and slapping his parents, who seemed completely incapable of coping with their son's rage. "It is an odd day when he does not break something," his father would write during William's toddler years.

In 1913, the Shockleys moved to Palo Alto and lived in a small house at 959 Waverley Street. Economic instability and his parents' obsession for complete privacy later led to a series of relocations from one downtown home to another. In Palo Alto, William's temper improved little at first. But ignoring psychiatric recommendations for more socialization, his parents decided to home school William until age eight. Finally, feeling they were unable to keep him out of a school setting any longer, they sent him to the Homer Avenue School for two years, where his

The house on Waverley Street in Palo Alto in which Shockley spent time as a child.
[PHOTO: MATT BOWLING]

Subtitle quotation from the 1967 Buffalo Springfield song, "For What It's Worth."

behavior improved dramatically—he even earned an "A" in comportment in his first year. As a teenager, William received more discipline at the Palo Alto Military Academy. As his biographer Joel Shurkin says, "Bill had learned to control his temper out in the world, saving it for [his parents] where it was most useful." After his father's death in 1925, he and his mother moved to Hollywood where William eventually entered Caltech to pursue a degree in physics.

After earning his Ph.D. from MIT and gaining employment at prestigious Bell Labs, the New Jersey research wing of AT&T, Shockley's plans would be sidetracked by Pearl Harbor. But his accomplishments in the next three-plus war years were astounding. It has been said that he saved thousands of lives without ever leaving his desk, mostly through his work advancing Allied techniques for using radar equipment and depth charges. Later, he completely redesigned the training procedures for American bomber crews. Near the end of the war, he became an expert consultant to the office of the Secretary of War—making him one of the highest ranked civilian scientists outside of Los Alamos. Remarkably, even before the war had begun, he and colleague James Fisk, quite by accident, designed a nuclear reactor similar to the Manhattan Project discovery that would lead to the atomic bomb. For all his war efforts, Shockley was awarded the National Medal of Merit.

Returning to Ma Bell after the war, Shockley was placed at the head of the 34-man Solid State Physics Team, where Shockley oversaw a team of brilliant physicists including John Bardeen and Walter H. Brattain. Their task: to find a smaller and reliable alternative to the fragile and bulky glass vacuum tube amplifiers that would not allow for a decent coast-to-coast call. Often sitting at a blackboard, trading theories and hypotheses, Shockley's team used what he would later call "creative failure methodology." After a series of trial and error setbacks and detours, Bardeen and Brattain finally broke through during the "magic month" of December 1947, inventing what would come to be called the transistor. And while Bell Labs quite rightly gave Shockley full credit as team leader, he would spend the next few years fuming over having had to learn of the great discovery over the phone.

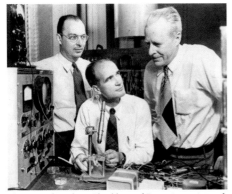

The team of Bardeen, Shockley and Brattain as pictured in 1948. [WIKIPEDIA COMMONS/AT&T, JACK ST.]

After the discovery, Shockley worked tirelessly to add to the invention. In his efforts, he invented an even stronger amplifying device—the junction transistor—and then forged ahead to author what would become the seminal work of his field, *Electrons and Holes in Semiconductors,* published in 1950.

The Shockley transistor would lead to other advances in transistor technology, eventually creating a vast new industry that sat at the heart of all modern electronics. As Joel Shurkin writes, "Shockley's feat… was his life's greatest accomplishment. It changed the world." Shockley then headed west to make some money off his invention—opening a shop at 391 San Antonio Road in Mountain View, essentially Silicon Valley's first startup. He had an eye for talent and since none of his Bell Labs colleagues would join him (he had by then ostracized Bardeen, Brattain and most of the others), Shockley hired the best and the brightest from nearby engineering schools.

But Shockley's managerial style would prove severe and suspicious. Eventually, the paranoia would lead to the 1957 defection of the so-called "Treacherous Eight," who fled Shockley Transistor to form rival Fairchild Semiconductor—eventually producing the first integrated circuits and beating their former boss to the punch. Many of the "Treacherous Eight" would later start spinoff companies, including Intel and National Semiconductor, ushering in the next generation of Silicon Valley. They would also manage to get rich while Shockley's company tanked.

In the 1960s after taking a professorship at Stanford University, Shockley became nearly obsessed with genetics—a field in which he was untrained, but about which he had become incredibly passionate. In 1965, he preached at a conference that the human race was threatened by a "genetic deterioration" and the attention he received from a *U.S. News & World Report* interview a month later further fueled his desire for verbal combat. His views became increasingly controversial, as he asserted that darker races were mentally inferior to whites and that ghetto blacks were "downbreeding" humanity. He became a firm proponent of eugenics: the belief that targeted breeding could lead to improvements in the human race.

Controversy and rage followed him everywhere and he welcomed it. He was the subject of rallies where he was called the "Hitler of the '80s." His classes and speeches were frequently interrupted by protesters, and he once debated face-to-face with Stanford protesters who burned him in effigy. By 1982, Shockley was running for the California Republican Party's Senate nomination on a platform advocating voluntary sterilization for those with an IQ under 100. He would finish in eighth place with less than one percent of the vote.

In 1989, Shockley would die in disgrace at the age of 79. He was all alone except for his second wife, Emmy, who did not hold funeral services because no one would have attended. His two children learned of his death by reading the newspaper.

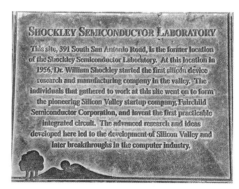

Street plaque marking location Shockley Semiconductor Laboratory at 391 South San Antonio Road, Mountain View. [PHOTO: BRIAN GEORGE]

Russel V. A. Lee, circa early 1970s

RUSSEL V. A. LEE
It's a Wonderful Life

PERHAPS NO PALO ALTAN HAS HAD A LIFE AS RICH OR FULL AS RUSSEL V. A. LEE, PALO Alto's most celebrated doctor. Remembering his time, one is reminded of Ben Franklin or Leonardo Da Vinci—men who tried their hand at virtually everything, seemingly unencumbered by time, money or the limitations of ordinary lives. In medicine—his primary passion—he paid little attention to accepted practice, rewriting the rules and then sitting back to watch with pleasure as the rest of the medical community caught up with him. And despite his enormous stature in the medical world, at times his doctoring seemed just one of his countless hobbies. Dr. Lee was also real estate mogul, devoted conservationist, amateur airplane pilot, big-time book collector, Stanford professor, champion poker player, prominent author, even world-record-holding fisherman—having caught a 435-pound tuna in Peru in 1957. By the time he died in 1982, Lee seemed to have crammed centuries of living into his 86 years on earth.

In 1895, Russel Van Arsdale Lee was born in Spanish Fork, Utah, to a rebellious minister who had moved west to convert Mormons to Calvinism. Russel moved to Palo Alto at age 16—with just eight dollars to his name—enrolling at Stanford University while earning his tuition fees by waiting tables at a Japanese restaurant. Later Russel held the unenviable position of examining the stools of Mother Lode miners for hookworms, one of many odd jobs that Lee had in his early life.

After getting his degree from Stanford Medical School, Lee began what would become a 42-year career teaching medicine at the university. Meanwhile, after marriage and a few years in San Francisco, he went into private practice in Palo Alto with Dr. Tom Williams in 1924. Five years later, Lee joined with five other doctors to form one of the first group practices in the

The Roth Building, Dr. Lee's professional home.
[PHOTO: BRIAN GEORGE]

Dr. Lee posing with Palo Alto architect Birge Clark.
[PHOTO: CAROLYN CADDES, CIRCA 1976]

country: the Palo Alto Clinic. Later, Lee would oversee the Clinic's growth into an arm of the Palo Alto Medical Foundation, today one of the country's largest multi-specialty practices.

In the 1930s, Lee was an early critic of Nazi Germany, sometimes sheltering war refugees in his own home. After Pearl Harbor, he served as a major, colonel and chief of preventive medicine in the Air Corps, as well as the personal physician for the U.S. Secretary of War. As part of his duties, he travelled to every front in the war.

After the war, Lee got into hot water as a delegate to the rather conservative American Medical Association (AMA). The group saw Lee's advocacy of group medical practice as heresy and his support of prepaid health care as socialist. But as with so many of the battles of his early life, Lee eventually proved to be ahead of his time. The AMA came around to supporting group medical care and, as Lee boasted in 1978, "most of the ideas that got me into great trouble with the AMA are now AMA policy."

But support for group practice was not Lee's only controversial belief. He was an early advocate of the prevention of venereal disease, actually writing the legislation for California's VD law that would establish a California bureau to fight sexual diseases. He even managed to usher it into law, lobbying the state legislature with $8,000 he had won in a high-stakes poker game.

Lee was also an early backer of legal abortions, the right to die, birth control and drug legalization. Sometimes he seemed to relish being at the center of controversy. Generating negative publicity in the 1960s, Lee argued that "the best way to solve our narcotics problem is to give dope addicts all the narcotics that they need." Although this remark was backed by an intelligent explanation of proposed policy, Lee was often just as happy to stir up trouble with flip remarks. He claimed to have received over 2,500 letters when opining that "considering a man as he is, as a mammal, monogamous marriage is a bizarre and unnatural state."

But behind the controversy, Lee was an exceptional doctor with a brilliant medical mind. Big ideas seemed to constantly pour out of him and many would eventually become reality. Realizing the need for a home for local medical research, Lee developed the Palo Alto Medical Research Foundation. Later pursuing his interest in the field of geriatrics, he was the leading force behind the establishment of Palo Alto's Channing House in 1962. Sometimes called "the finest retirement home in the country," Channing House's innovative arrangement in which residents buy into lifetime medical care is still in place 45 years after its founding.

Lee also served with distinction on President Truman's Commission on the Health Needs of the Nation in 1951. As such, he was an early advocate of national health insurance and later devised a plan that became Medicare—again earning the displeasure of the AMA.

A strong advocate of affordable health care, Lee lamented in his later years that medical care was still too expensive—even at his own clinic. But he was also proud to say that he never made money off of his patients. It was through real estate that Lee amassed a fortune. Buying land around Palo Alto and Portola Valley, he became a millionaire when prices skyrocketed. Later, he secured his position with environmentalists when he and his wife Dorothy rejected developers and donated and sold 1,400 acres of land to the City of Palo Alto for its renowned Foothills Park.

Later in life, the goateed, always elegant good doctor became a kind of Biblical patriarch—his house surrounded by those of four of his children, all of whom became doctors. After losing his wife Dorothy in 1972 and his only daughter the following year, Lee's elder years were sustained by his remaining family. The compound became home to most of his 21 grandchildren and eventually five great-grandchildren. His house itself became something of a shrine to a lifetime of hobbies. Inside was a 15,000-volume library full of first editions and thirteenth century rarities, more than 150 chess sets picked up during his six trips around the world, and a basement full of wine made in his own vineyards.

And in his '80s, Lee wrote a book about how to age gracefully—the appropriately titled *No Gravy on the Vest,* in which he explained how to avoid slowing down. And Dr. Lee certainly retained his youthful attitude into his declining years. Asked at 84 what he wanted to do with the rest of his life, the smiling Lee responded that his greatest ambition was "to lose a paternity suit."

Weeks before his death, he told his close friend Robert Jamplis, "Bobby, I'm tired… my locomotion is poor and my memory is failing. It is time I left this old world and I only hope it will be soon, swift and painless." No longer able to live life at full throttle, Russel Lee's final day came on January 27, 1982. Later that week, 600 of his friends showed up to honor the man with the earthy humor who had changed the field of medicine. His longtime colleague William Clark eulogized, "My many contacts with this man of unbelievable energy, brilliant intellect and far-sighted imagination were always stimulating, at times exasperating and never dull."

A photo montage showing an aerial view of Channing House, an enduring Russel Lee creation.

Jerry Garcia performing with the Grateful Dead, New Haven, CT. WPLR Show. [WIKIPEDIA COMMONS/PHOTO: CARL LENDER]

THE GRATEFUL DEAD
Making the Scene in Palo Alto

"Palo Alto was the magic carpet. It was where everything happened. That's where the music was… Jerry [Garcia] was there and [Bob] Hunter was there… all the characters were there. Palo Alto was the beautiful golden basket that this all came out of… Palo Alto was INCREDIBLE in those days."—Carolyn "Mountain Girl" Garcia.

In the late 1950s and early 1960s, those years when the American counterculture was slowly moving from Beatnik intellectualism towards psychedelic hippiedom, Palo Alto was a pretty happening place. This is rather surprising, because in those years the city was far more conservative and less urban than it is today—after all, Palo Alto was still basically dry until 1971. But in this quasi-university town not too far from San Francisco, a youth scene sprouted up on the city's liberal fringes that would end up producing some big-time artists, including the Kingston Trio, Joan Baez and the very symbol of American counterculture—the Grateful Dead.

In 1960, 18-year-old Jerry Garcia arrived in Palo Alto. The future Grateful Dead leader had just been discharged from an unlikely Army stint where he had accrued two courts-martial and eight AWOLs. At the time, the daytime center of literary and intellectual activity for Palo Alto youth was actually in Menlo Park at Kepler's Books on El Camino. Still in operation today, Kepler's was a kind of hypercreative living room for what Garcia's then-girlfriend Barbara Meier would later say was a full-time "collection of poets, musicians, painters, writers, socialists and pacifists, with a smattering of out-and-out lunatics." Garcia took up nearly daily residence as part of the Kerouac-inspired, neo-Beatnik crowd hanging out in Kepler's backroom.

At night, the action tended to shift over to St. Michael's Alley, a funky Palo Alto coffee shop at 436 University which had launched Joan Baez a couple years earlier. There were other places

The Grateful Dead in their post-PA years at Ocean Beach, San Francisco, 1967. [PHOTO: HERBIE GREENE]

The Top of the Tangent, at the corner of University Avenue and the "Circle" in Palo Alto, a hang-out of the band that would become the Grateful Dead, is in the upper floor of the building to the right in this photo.

University Avenue at Kipling Street where Swain's House of Music once stood. Swain's once rented instruments to the Warlocks, the original Grateful Dead.

as well—the Top of the Tangent, a small folk club upstairs from a pizza parlor at 117 University Avenue, and The Chateau, a three-story, old Victorian house on Santa Cruz Avenue in Menlo Park that approached the atmosphere of a hippie commune. Later the scene would shift to author Ken Kesey's house on Perry Lane, near Stanford Golf Course, and to a huge turn-of-the-century Victorian at 436 Hamilton Avenue in downtown Palo Alto.

Indeed, reading accounts of the Dead's formative years is like a walk through Palo Alto in the early 1960s. For example, Garcia was in bandmate Bob Weir's apartment on High Street, thumbing through a Funk & Wagnalls Dictionary, when he came up with the Grateful Dead name. Garcia's wedding to Sara Ruppenthal took place on April 25, 1963 at the Unitarian Church, followed by a reception at Ricky's Garden Hotel.

Garcia met eventual Grateful Dead bassist Phil Lesh and keyboardist "Pigpen" McKernan at Palo Alto parties, and for a while Garcia and longtime Dead lyricist Robert Hunter lived side by side in their cars in a nearby lot. The early version of the Dead, the Warlocks, rented their instruments from Swain's House of Music at 451 University. When he encountered Bob Weir, Garcia had a job as a guitar and banjo teacher at Dana Morgan Music on Bryant Street. But while Garcia earlier may have been totally immersed in the Palo Alto scene, he was basically free floating and free loading until his life was jolted by a terrific car crash on the night of February 20, 1961.

At around one in the morning, after a party at The Chateau, Garcia went out for a drive with three friends—Alan Trist, Paul Speegle and Lee Adams, who was behind the wheel of a 1956 Studebaker Golden Hawk. The car was up to nearly 90 mph on Junipero Serra Boulevard when it jumped the guardrail, flipped over several times and landed on top of Speegle, killing him instantly. All the passengers were thrown from the car, including Garcia, who literally came out of his shoes. The three survivors ended up at Stanford Hospital with Garcia sporting a broken collarbone. Later he would say that the crash was "where my life began. Before then I was always living at less than capacity. I was idling. That was the slingshot for the rest of my life."

By early 1964, after a rather unsuccessful attempt at married life and a cross-country trip to find the roots of his beloved bluegrass music, Garcia began his move toward forming the Grateful Dead. On New Year's Eve 1963, Garcia had met 15-year-old Bob Weir, future Grateful Dead guitarist, who later described the encounter: "I was wandering the back streets of Palo Alto with a friend when we heard banjo music coming from the back of a music store… It was Garcia waiting for his pupils, unmindful it was New Year's Eve. We sat down and started jamming and had a great old rave. I had my guitar with me and we played a little and decided to start a jug band."

The jug band was Mother McCree's Uptown Jug Champions, Garcia's nod to the niche of folk music that took off as a minor craze in the early 1960s. But despite his love of banjos, jugs and bluegrass, Garcia found that playing "old-timey" folk in Palo Alto was not so easy. After 25 or 30 gigs over the course of eight months, Jerry began to move toward cutting-edge rock 'n' roll. Pulling him hard in that direction was the soaring phenomenon of the Beatles.

In 1964, the American musical world was turned upside down by the British invasion of the Beatles. As Garcia's biographer Blair Jackson put it, "Like half of America under the age of 25, Jerry had been seduced by the Beatles, especially their film "A Hard Day's Night" which depicted life as a rock 'n' roll band as just about as much fun as you could have on Planet Earth." Bob Weir agreed, "The Beatles were why we turned from a jug band into a rock 'n' roll band. What we saw them do was impossibly attractive." Plus, Garcia had forever fallen in love with the electric guitar.

As Garcia and Weir turned toward rock 'n' roll, Mother McCree's evolved into the harder-rocking Warlocks. The new lineup featured Garcia, Bob Weir, Dana Morgan, Jr. (from the Bryant Street music store) on bass, Bill Kreutzmann (from Paly's best band, The Legends) on drums and Paly dropout Ron "Pigpen" McKernan on keyboards and harmonica.

Over the next few years, as the Warlocks officially became the Grateful Dead, the band rose to ever greater heights. As LSD and hallucinatory drugs infused the Palo Alto scene, author Ken Kesey and his band of Merry Pranksters began to stage elaborate drug parties dubbed Acid Tests in Palo Alto and other California cities. The Grateful Dead essentially became the house band of the Acid Tests, furthering their reputation and reach. Soon they were off to Haight-Ashbury and eventual stardom as the Grateful Dead became the most iconic counterculture band of the 1960s. They would end up the greatest and highest grossing live music band in history.

Along the way the Dead acquired an insanely devoted following of fans—nicknamed Deadheads— who worshipped the band for decades and followed them on their "endless tour." Even today, some 2,314 concerts later and long after Garcia's fatal heart attack in 1995, Deadheads still scour the internet looking for old mementos of the band. It seems sure that some still hope to find a piece of that magic carpet from the Grateful Dead's earliest days, back when "Palo Alto… was where everything happened."

Bob Weir performing with Kingfish, 1975.
[WIKIPEDIA COMMONS/PHOTO: DAVID GANS]

Ruse by truck

Beatles foil fans on exit

By KEITH HEARN

England's weary Beatles — George, John, Paul and Ringo — slipped out of Palo Alto's Cabana Motor Hotel by 1½-ton rented truck this morning and sneaked aboard a London-bound jet liner at San Francisco International Airport an hour late all to the dismay of nearly 500 restless young fans.

They'd arrived at the Cabana at 10:30 p.m. Tuesday by sleek black limousine after two performances at Daly City's Cow Palace before a total of 28,000 screaming, yelling, surging fans, mostly teen-age girls.

Today, the foursome slipped away at 10:46 a.m. in an elaborate maneuver while newsmen, fans and Cabana employes were looking the other way.

Four hundred fans anxiously awaited their departure from the front entrance, but they left by the same back entrance through which they'd entered the night before.

Announced plans for today's departure were to rush the Beatles down the northside elevator, whisk them through inside corridors past the Cabana's kitchen and out through the service entrance.

Two decoy limousines were sent out ahead of a closed truck that many fans thought contained what they had been waiting to see. They waved goodbye.

But on the south side of the hotel a rented truck was waiting. Policemen gave the high sign to fellow officers on an eighth-floor window. Moments later, the smiling long-hairs bustled out of the elevator into the driveway.

"Where's the car?" asked Paul McCartney, Beatle guitarist.

"Here, better get in now," said a police sergeant, pointing to the truck.

"Oh, the same lorry again," McCartney answered, referring to a similar truck which Tuesday afternoon spirited the group from International Airport to the Cow Palace.

In piled McCartney, plus John Lennon and George Harrison.

The truck lurched forward but stopped four feet away — they'd forgotten drummer Ringo Starr and manager Brian Epstein. After they clanked through the chain-link-and canvas cover the truck zipped away unnoticed by the crowd in front looking the other way.

A half-dozen girls who had happened to see the secret loading maneuver chased the truck out and screamed the alert to the crowd, but the white-and-blue van had already passed.

September 1, 1965
[PALO ALTO TIMES]

BEATLEMANIA INVADES PALO ALTO
A Celebrity Story

EVERYONE LIKES A CELEBRITY STORY—THE TIME THEY SAW ELTON JOHN COMING OUT OF a deli or nearly sharing an elevator with John Travolta. While such celebrity encounters aren't usually all that eventful, they are rarely forgotten by the storyteller—a brief moment in the glow of a big-time star. Sometimes cities have celebrity stories too, and Palo Alto has a good one.

Of course, it's not as if Palo Alto has never known famous people. In the 1940s, romance novelist and Palo Alto resident Kathleen Norris was a household name nationwide. And these days either Steve Jobs or Steve Young could both be considered "Most Famous Palo Altan"—depending on whether your interests range toward geek or jock. But Palo Alto's biggest brush with the rich and famous certainly came on August 31, 1965—when Beatlemania came to town.

In the 1960s, the Cabaña Hotel was a minor celebrity hotspot out on El Camino Real. Built with Vegas flair, the Cabaña seemed a little out of place in Palo Alto. But the far-flung locale was perfect for the concerting Beatles, who by 1965 were more than a little fatigued from out-running their rabidly lovesick fan base. Following a twin concert at the Cow Palace in San Francisco, the Fab Four were "sequestered" down in Palo Alto, looking for a little peace and quiet.

Still, even in Palo Alto, the Beatles weren't exactly strolling down University Avenue. Some 3,000 fans, mostly female, crowded into the Cabaña parking lot (some overnight) along with the screaming, crying and emotional breakdowns that seemed to follow the foursome everywhere. Out-of-control fans passed the Cabaña's outlandish replicas of the David and the Venus De Milo, swarmed across El Camino Real (backing up traffic) and into the Rickey's lot across the street. A few girls even slipped past the guards and actually began to climb up the outer grating of the hotel (presumably with the goal of reaching the Beatles) before being coaxed down.

The Beatles' invasion in 1964.
[WIKIPEDIA COMMONS/U.S. LIBRARY OF CONGRESS/UP INTERNATIONAL]

Police were everywhere. It cost the county sheriff's office some $11,000 to provide 80 men and 30 patrol cars for the Beatles' 25-hour stay. Palo Alto itself shelled out some $700 in overtime in order to station officers at the Cabaña and the hotel's security bill was $4,000 after hiring 200 temporary security guards, including players from the University of Santa Clara football team.

But most of the action occurred as the Beatles came and went. Upon arrival, the scene of pandemonium outside the Cabaña resembled one of the frantic free-for-alls displayed the year before in their film, "A Hard Day's Night." Fans climbed onto the Beatles limousine, rocking the car and denting the roof. Years later, one Beatle fan recalled that upon getting out, this most famous rock group in music history simply looked like "four scared kids."

The next morning, however, the Beatles made a slick getaway. Plans were announced that the Beatles were to be whisked out of their Room 810 Suite, down the northside elevator, past the Cabaña kitchen and out through the service entrance. Sure enough, two decoy limos and a truck

The Cabana Hotel in its more eccentric days.
[THE CAROLYN PIERCE POSTCARD COLLECTION]

were stationed out front, prompting many fans to wave goodbye to Beatles that they mistakenly thought were inside. Instead, the boys were sent by police out the southside entrance. "Where's the car?" asked Paul, upon arriving—only to be directed into a white and blue 1.5-ton delivery truck along with John and George.

But as the truck frantically made its way for the Cabaña exit, the driver realized he had left Ringo behind—not the last time the Beatle drummer would feel forgotten—and had to slam on the brakes to let in the fourth band member. A photograph of two of Palo Alto female fans—14-year-old Rocky Keith and 13-year-old Sue Moore—was printed in the *Palo Alto Times* the next day "sobbing with joy" because they happened to see the Beatles exit. But most of the girls on the other side of the hotel were not so lucky—and were forced to console themselves by later purchasing pieces of Beatle bedsheets sold in the Cabaña parking lot.

The Cow Palace show itself was even rowdier as 28,000 crazed fans twisted and shouted to a 31-minute concert. Before even taking the stage, one teenage girl burst through security and threw herself at the band. And during the show, more than 100 girls ran for the platform, and a half-dozen girls actually made it to the group. One 14-year-old dived for John and as she was being dragged off stage was heard screaming, "I'm Michelle, I'm Michelle, you just don't know at all, John, I want to die here with you!"

At one point, the performance was halted for some 10 minutes as Paul pleaded with the unruly throng to allow police to remove a pregnant woman who had fainted. She was just one of dozens of girls who became dazed or unconscious during the show and were taken to first-aid stations. Later, the crowd became so frenzied that it took a line of newsmen to lock arms in front of the stage to prevent the band from being completely overrun.

By 1966, the band decided it was through with the craziness that accompanied their live performances. After a final Candlestick Park performance on August 29, 1966, the Beatles would never tour again.

Today, the Beatles' brief stay in Palo Alto is still remembered in the remodeled Crowne Plaza Cabaña. Room 810 has been named the "Beatles Room" and the walls are decorated with images of Paul jumping into the delivery truck and the band posing in the Cabaña lobby. For the Beatles, their stay in Palo Alto must have been one of hundreds of stops in a blur of limos, hotels and narrow escapes. But for Palo Alto's teenagers of the 1960s it remains their great celebrity story.

The caption to this photo taken at the Cabaña, September 1, 1965, read, "On the outside looking in."
[PALO ALTO TIMES]

The Superpig leaflet, 1972.

JIM ZURCHER
Chief Superpig

Things got personal in the demonstration battles of the 1960s and early '70s, when student protesters were pitted against the nation's young cops. The students, largely from white-collar suburban homes, were inspired by a cultural and civil rights movement that promised to change the country. On the other side, newly hired police officers saw themselves as the thin blue line protecting their communities from the increasing chaos and disorder. There was little common ground between the two groups. Students characterized the police as uneducated pigs with a penchant for giving beatings, while most cops saw the students as privileged, spoiled drop-outs just looking to cause trouble. Tensions ran high in every encounter.

Jim Zurcher, who took over as police chief in 1971, tried to diffuse those tensions in Palo Alto. A folk guitar player, marathon runner and possibly the best pistol-shooting police chief in the country, Zurcher would attempt to bridge the gap between police and protesters. It would bring him both hearty praise and heavy criticism.

A firm believer in both the letter of the law and First Amendment rights, 37-year-old Zurcher brought a new tolerance and broad-mindedness to an old-guard police force. By the time he retired 16 years later, the Palo Alto Police Department was a different organization—more open, diverse, and responsive to the community. But it wouldn't come easy. Many of his policies struck at the heart of what older officers saw as the essence of police work. And in his first months on the job, the relationship between the Palo Alto police and Stanford student protesters reached a new low.

On April 9, 1971, Stanford students and other protesters staged a violent sit-in, barricading themselves inside the Stanford Medical Center to protest the firing of black custodian Sam Bridges. After a 30-hour occupation, the PAPD surrounded the demonstrators and attempted

Chief Zurcher, AKA the "Superpig."

Jim Zurcher with his beloved Gibson guitar.

After the Superpig controversy, Zurcher went to a drawing of this haloed cop instead.

to batter down the door. But the officers were blindsided by protesters wielding chair legs, iron clubs, and a relentless fire hose. Zurcher later called it "the most vicious and unprovoked attack on police I have ever witnessed."

In the fracas, 13 cops were injured, two of them seriously. The incident augmented the already heightened tension between protesters and police. Yet it seemed to give Zurcher new resolve to find mutual understanding. Still settling into his office, the new chief sought to change attitudes within the department and the image the PAPD projected to the outside community.

Inside the department, Zurcher pursued the type of systemic changes bound to cause internal division. In his first months, Zurcher replaced the old paramilitary command organization with a more progressive team-management approach. He sent cops for training in conflict management, saying that the police were there to "mediate disputes, not merely to ticket and arrest"—an opinion that did not please some of his older officers. He also favored crime prevention methods and theories of community policing which were seen as rather avant-garde in those days. Zurcher later said he put hard-nosed officers with a reputation for beating and harassing demonstrators on the midnight "graveyard shift," while shifting many discontented officers to other jobs. Some veterans simply retired rather than accept the department's new doctrine.

Zurcher's proudest accomplishment was bringing women into the Palo Alto police force. He gets credit for hiring Palo Alto's first female cop (1971), first female lieutenant (1982) and first female captain (1985)—changes for which he received little support from his own officers at the time. He also furthered gains by Palo Alto's black, Hispanic and Asian officers.

Meanwhile, Zurcher tried to reach out to the protesters, saying that he saw the police "as advocates of the people, instead of adversaries." In an attempt to humanize his own force, he took to drawing himself in a non-human form. At a 1972 demonstration against Deputy Defense Secretary David Packard, demonstrators received leaflets showing the chief as the "Superpig," a cartoon swine wearing the chief's badge and flashing the peace sign. Using the radicals' most incendiary name-calling epithet in a little old fashioned reverse psychology, Zurcher attempted to turn the tables on the police-protester relationship. As he said later, "The protesters always leafleted everyone else, so I thought, why not leaflet them?"

The pamphlet contained some "suggestions for peaceful demonstration from Palo Alto's Superpig." It stated that "If the President and the leaders of the People's Republic of China can normalize relations between two opposing philosophies, I'm sure we can cooperate to carry on a peaceful demonstration. We are here to insure the safety of all those present. That includes those wishing to demonstrate peacefully. We ask that you let our officers guide your march and assist you in crossing any streets."

Naturally, there was a backlash from the department's old guard. One of his officers called it "highly unprofessional for a chief to label himself 'super pig.' It makes us piglets… We fail to see any humor or levity in it." Zurcher later apologized, opting instead for the image of a smiling cartoon chief with a hovering halo. But his earlier cartoon visage was forever immortalized when the Zurcher "Superpig" became the subject of a song on a Cleveland radio station.

And Zurcher's original thinking wasn't just limited to cartoon illustrations. He also brought innovative ideas to potentially dangerous situations. When radical left-wing Venceremos members were accused of aiding in a murder, they holed themselves up inside a house on Channing Avenue. The San Bernardino Sheriff's department, with plans to break down the door, was gearing up for a potentially deadly shoot-out. But Zurcher had the house surrounded with cops and successfully talked the suspects out without a shot fired. Not to say that he wasn't tough. Zurcher established effective Embarcadero Road speed traps, closed down prostitution houses disguised as massage parlors and cracked down on local burglars in South Palo Alto.

He also stood by his officers' right in 1971 to raid the *Stanford Daily's* press offices looking for photographic evidence against the Medical Center attackers—although the decision to enter the newspaper headquarters was made without his authorization. The paper sued the department and the case went all the way to the Supreme Court before the PAPD won.

Since Zurcher was the head of the police force, the case became known as Zurcher vs. *Stanford Daily,* ironically branding the chief's name on the conservative side of a case found today in every law school textbook. After being portrayed in national editorial cartoons as a Gestapo-like gun wielding brute, Zurcher took to wearing a T-shirt proclaiming "I am not an ogre."

By the time Zurcher retired in 1987 as Palo Alto's top cop, much had changed in both the city and the country. A calmer tide of history had washed away much of the bad blood between the PAPD and the community. Still, looking back on the progressive policies that have become standard Palo Alto police practice, there is no doubt that the innovations of the "Chief Superpig" played a major role.

An "End the War" demonstration along University Avenue during the late 1960s.

Greg Brown at work. [PHOTO: CAROLYN CADDES]

GREG BROWN: MURALS & PUBLIC ART
Fueling the Imagination in Palo Alto

G OVERNMENT RARELY PUTS FORWARD A FUNNY FACE. THERE'S OBVIOUSLY NOT MUCH humor in your typical letter from the IRS or in the driver license renewal process, but public art and civic architecture tend to be serious business. Monumental courthouses and statehouses with Corinthian columns, raking cornices, and heroic statues superimpose a rather lofty expression on the face of government. When it comes to public art, the powers that be often tilt toward modern sculptures that stand in front of city buildings with a kind of overblown gravity.

Perhaps it's the wink at solemnity that's the brilliance of the beloved Greg Brown murals. Encountered here and there in the nooks and crannies of Palo Alto, they are deceptively simple, funny and full of surprise. And over the years they have become part of the experience of living in Palo Alto. It's heartening to know that our city government not only gave the initial approval for these murals but has tried to protect them over the years. When you can look up on a faceless concrete building in Palo Alto and see a mural of green aliens climbing up a stairway to hug a milkman—well, that's the kind of city I want to live in.

Greg Brown's work is possibly the only truly popular public art in the city. Brown grew up in town, yet it took both the public Art Commission and the U.S. Congress to bring his whimsical contradictions to local walls. Palo Alto made art in public places a civic promise in 1975, but it was a federal jobs program that funded Brown's early murals. His first mural in Palo Alto came in 1975, when as an artist in residence he earned $4.75 an hour decorating a wall of the Mitchell Park Skating Rink. Soon he was at work on the Palo Alto Pedestrian Series, a collection of *trompe-l'oeil* murals of aliens, pelicans, milkmen, regular folks and ne'er-do-wells. Later, when some of his murals were slated for destruction due to building demolitions and remodeling, there was a

An alien makes a wrong turn into what is now the Comerica Bank on Lytton. [PHOTO: MATT BOWLING]

This Greg Brown mural no longer exists.

hue and cry from the citizenry. The City Council worked with businesses to save the murals, and Brown offered to repaint a couple on new buildings.

These days six of the original nine city commissions are still around to intrigue pedestrians and raise a smile. Along with several privately funded additions, the murals add to the pleasure of a city stroll and remind the busy, overstressed errand-runner to slow down and not take life too seriously. The murals catch you at odd moments. On the way into Restoration Hardware, you glimpse an older gentleman, possibly Spiro Agnew, pushing a baby alien in a stroller. On your way to withdraw cash at Comerica Bank, you notice that an alien ship has crash-landed into the side wall. And heading into the elevator at 261 Hamilton, you are startled by a man with an evil grin preparing to cut the elevator cables.

It's not as if Palo Alto's citizen critics are that easy to please. Feelings ran so high over a design to replace the fountain on California Avenue that the Art Commission withdrew its original choice and invited input through an online poll. And many other works of public art have provoked outspoken opinion. Some are thought pretentious, others just bizarre. California Avenue has an assortment of controversial and esoteric pieces. Statues include "Go Mama," a six-foot bronze sculpture of a Mexican doll with a face in its belly, "Jungle Jane," a nine-foot aluminum wire face and "Body of the Urban Myth," a privately commissioned 12-foot ancient Greek woman hoisting a washing machine. A trip around Palo Alto can sometimes seem like a gallery walk. Ponder an oversized green egg in Lytton Plaza known as "Digital DNA," a car with legs in Bowden Park called "Rrrun" or a steel "Tilted Donut" at El Camino and Page Mill.

A number of other public pieces have suffered the ultimate in critical wrath—outright vandalism. The artist who designed "Digital DNA" once suggested planting a video camera inside the egg to stem the tide of vandalism. And the wooden sculpture "Foreign Friends" that sat at Waverley and Embarcadero ultimately perished. A gift from Palo Alto's Swedish sister city, the oversized painted couple sitting on a park bench with their dog met a rather unfriendly fate. In less than a decade, the piece was ridiculed, smashed, sawed, splashed with paint, set on fire, and twice decapitated. It was once even bedecked with a large, fully addressed postcard inscribed with the words "Return to Sender." Tough audience indeed.

As it turns out, strong opinions are nothing new. Way back in 1932, long before the days of city-sponsored art, one of Palo Alto's first public exposures to modern painting produced both squawking and gawking from the community. The cause was found at the entrance to the newly built Palo Alto Medical Clinic, where a series of Art Deco frescoes celebrated modern medicine. Dr. Russel Lee commissioned them from Victor Arnautoff, a Russian-born muralist who had worked with Diego Rivera in both Mexico and San Francisco and who later would work on the WPA-funded murals in Coit Tower. Arnautoff created eight panels contrasting modern medical practice with outmoded methods of the past.

But it wasn't medical techniques which caught the public's attention, it was the human body. A woman naked above the waist is examined by a gray-bearded doctor with a stethoscope. A semi-nude male patient looks, as one writer put it, "as nonchalant as though a clinic held no more terrors than a Turkish bath." A bare-breasted woman is saved from devils by an ancient witch doctor. And it didn't take the press long to suggest that shocking paintings were on view at the new clinic. True, some people were disturbed by the partly nude figures, and the *San Francisco Chronicle* had condescending fun with the story, but public reaction in Palo Alto seems to have leaned more toward curiosity than puritanical outrage. On the Sunday following the unveiling, bumper-to-bumper traffic backed up on Homer Avenue as drivers detoured from their usual scenic routes to take in the newsworthy images. The result was Palo Alto's first traffic jam.

Stroll along Homer today and you can see that the murals were left intact when the clinic moved, in 1999, to larger quarters on El Camino Real. (If you visit the Medical Foundation's present location, notice vignettes of the historic murals that link the new building to the past.) At this writing, the original structure, now called the Roth Building and owned by the city, is poised for a new role. Once it is rehabilitated and reborn as the Palo Alto History Museum, the Arnautoff murals will be readily visible.

With such a distinctive past, can the restored building look forward to a new mural to celebrate its function as a history museum? The medical murals will still highlight the entrance. But step into adjacent Heritage Park and you'll see a sizable wall facing the park's long axis. Then imagine Greg Brown up there on a scaffold. His work is already part of local history, but with his encouragement the Palo Alto History Museum foresees a major new mural. With luck, the empty wall will be uniquely transformed by our homegrown muralist's view of Palo Alto history. As the time nears for restoration to begin, chances are good that Greg Brown's art will keep fueling the imaginations—and the comments—of Palo Altans far into the 21st century.

An unidentified man observes the graffiti on the "Foreign Friends" statue.

This was the most controversial painting on the Roth Building mural. [PALO ALTO MEDICAL FOUNDATION/FRED ENGLISH]

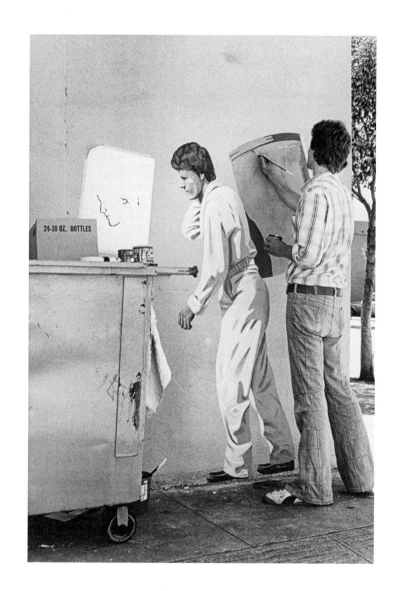

MORE...

About the Author

Matt Bowling is an historian, former second-grade teacher and the founder of the Palo Alto civics program for kids called Kidizens. He is also the author of two short books on Palo Alto history, *Nice Day for a Stroll* and *Palo Alto History for Kids*. In addition, he has created numerous websites including *Blizzardof78.org*, about his first memory—the great snowstorm that hit Boston when he was three—along with other educational and history websites such as *Superpridecards.org*, *ElectionWall.org* and *Debatestats.com*. He loves the Malian band Amadou & Miriam, the movie "Paper Moon" and best of all, playing with his 3-year-old daughter, Addie Luna.

Author, Matt Bowling, and his daughter, Addie Luna.
[PHOTO: MATT BOWLING]

The Palo Alto Historical Association

The Palo Alto Historical Association (PAHA), a non-profit organization, works to collect, preserve and make available to the public information about the history of Palo Alto through monthly newsletters and programs, publications and digital resources. In addition, the association maintains the Palo Alto Guy Miller Archives, a collection of letters, photographs, records and ephemera of which 12,000 items are currently digitized and 3,000 are on our website. All images reproduced in this book, unless specifically noted alongside the photograph, are from these archives.

We invite readers' interest and participation—if you want to know more about PAHA's work, wish to peruse the list of publications, attend the monthly programs, have an interest in pursuing local history scholarship, or want to become a member, please visit *www.pahistory.org*.

PUBLICATIONS COMMITTEE

Harriette Shakes
Chair/Book design

Steve Staiger
Historian

Betty Gerard
Editor-in-Chief

Brian George
Image Curator

Larry Christenson
Marketing

Chris Botsford
Treasurer

John Hackmann
Vice President/Programs

Doug Graham
President

Palo Alto Historical Association
Palo Alto, California